THE TEJ GUIDE TO PROPERTY INVESTING

Building a Profitable Property Business

Tej Singh

Tej Talks

First paperback edition Q4 2020

ISBN 9798558903584

tej-talks.com // tejinvests.com

Tej Talks

REVIEWS

Rob Hodge - @MaygreenInvestments
"I first met Tej back in 2018 and what first struck me about him was his thirst for knowledge and down to earth realism. What Tej has achieved in the time I've known him is quite frankly astonishing and this book is packed with the lessons he's had along the way. Tej owns his mistakes as much as he celebrates his successes and that shows in his character and the way he writes. If you want a book on the realities of property investing from ground zero, this is the book for you."

Mohit Mehta - @MVMPropertiesLtd
"This is not only a full guide that provides any novice investor a step by step guide from start to finish for everything they need to know, but one that is real and has come from someone who is actually investing in property right now. From the first page, Tej's personality shines through making it an enjoyable and very honest book. I myself, not as a novice investor, but one who has been investing for over 1.5 years, have taken away a lot of valuable information. I can't recommend this enough for investors – well done Tej! You have disrupted the market with this and will help many people avoid costly mistakes"

Ayaz Saboor - @SameDoorProperties
"This book provides a brilliant overview of the BRR strategy. It goes above and beyond the basic concepts and whets the appetite for you to go out and get hands on experience. Tej has a wealth of knowledge that he shares along with his mistakes. Great read and highly recommended for anyone starting out."

Anika Vaghela - @Anika_V

"The verdict? Incredible! Whether you're starting off in property or experienced, this book won't let you down. It's full of knowledge, expert advice and not to mention humour. Educational in the field of Buy, Refurbish, Refinance and one to keep aside for reference purposes. Genuinely can't rate this book highly enough!"

Rich Liddle - @Rich.Liddle

"I was pleased to be one of the first to read Tej's new book and I was hugely impressed by not only the content but also the clear and simplistic way he presented it. This really stood his book apart from others in this field as it was a pleasure to read rather than a chore, the information flowed in a logical order and is an absolute go to resource for anyone starting out, however, it is not only educational it is also a humorous and light hearted as it canters through the journey Tej embarked on as he grew his successful portfolio."

Rubi Takhar - @rubi_can_property

"It was an absolute pleasure to be one of the first to read Tej's new book. Being a beginner in property I can say this book covers everything you need to know to help get you started. It will be a 'go-to' guide for people I'm sure. Tej has done a great job of breaking down each section making it informative yet easy to understand, his humour and personality really shines through along the way which keeps you entertained and wanting to read more"

CONTENTS

"If it is not right do not do it;
if it is not true do not say it."
Marcus Aurelius

ABOUT ME

Tej Talks

I wasn't raised in poverty, I have never had credit card debt, I haven't had a major life event that's suddenly made me so passionate and driven to get into property. Oh no, how will I ever sell you a dream without an emotional hook at the start? Wait, let me think of an elaborate story, told slowly, with many pauses, and get you to raise your hands, about my long-lost uncle who left me £1m, which I then lost by betting on racing hamsters. Then the Mafia were after me and I just about escaped, and found financial freedom in exactly 3.47 weeks with no experience or money.

Forget that, I'll tell you who I really am.

I'm Tej, born in 1993 in West London. I was raised in a family that you would say is middle class, I never experienced money worries (I also didn't spend much). My mother is a head teacher, my father a photographer and I have one sister. Growing up my main challenge was anger; my parents divorced when I was about 9 and soon after I started to become insular and quiet, but very angry. My anger meant I never really had many friends, in High School I had 2 close friends, and I had fought with (often physically) many other people. This changed in Sixth form, then University, but really only shifted dramatically when I founded my Recruitment business at 23. I discovered Stoicism and it really changed my life. I slowly started to remove my Ego, understand my reality and that I created this anger, I let it run rampant. Therefore, as easy as I created it - I could stop it. I'm not a saint, but I've come a long way in controlling my emotions. I have to thank my fiancée and Mother for having a big impact on this too. We all have personal challenges like this, I share it with you, so you understand you're not alone and we all have our own unique past and experiences that shape us.

Fast forward to today and I spend most of my time in Property and Branding. What free time I have I spend it with my loved ones, cooking (I'm obsessed with Italy), learning languages (Español), reading and playing Xbox. I love understanding the world's cultures, the history, meaning and traditions that make Earth such a rich place. I love animals too. I love to dance; I've actually performed Bhangra at the Wembley Arena in front of 4,500 people!

That's me, what about my *professional experience*:

I studied Biochemistry at King's College London.

Good boy.

I then worked in Pharmaceuticals, after failing 40 interviews to get one job, I then got fired 8 months in.

Bad boy.

I wanted to work in an industry more ethical than Pharma… so I set up a Recruitment business, clearly the flagship of ethics that one. I ran this for 3.5 years, working from home mainly. I had my first placement (sale) in 2 weeks, and it was profitable ever since. In fact, profits almost doubled every year. I took minimal salary because I'd been raised to save money, and not to spend it on material items that are not necessary. I lived at home, so had no rent or bills or too much food to pay for, it was great.

I got very lonely and annoyed at the world. Everyone seems to hate recruiters, the second they realise who you are on the phone. I didn't start this to be disliked by people who don't know me, but I understand why they act like that. The industry has a bad name, and a lot of

Recruiters are bad, this is a challenge - one I didn't have the passion to want to overcome. That's okay sometimes, it means you're not doing the right thing. So, I continued with 'golden handcuffs', making money but not enjoying it. I then did some in-house contracting as I missed humans (and respect). It was the most fun I've ever had, I loved it, I got paid a lot of money too. £450 a day for many months, to do a job that I found easy and have a laugh all day? I'll have that!

I mention my salary, because I quit and turned it all down to have a pay of £0 a day and be a property investor. Why would I do that? Through Stoicism I realised the importance of money as a tool, a vehicle for freedom, a necessity, but my happiness is from within, not from cash. I needed to do something that drove me and would keep my going through the hard times and would build a 'Passive Income'.

During this contracting and prior to this, I was listening to property podcasts, subscribing to magazines, in Facebook groups, networking, reading books, buying people coffees/food to pick their brain and building my team. I did this for about six months, I thought I was making progress by doing like one viewing a week, if that. I started off trying Rent to Rent, which I soon gave up as it did not interest me, and I didn't need quick cash flow. Looking back, those 6 months were invaluable. They really set the foundations for my Property Business and Brand. You need the right foundations, don't skip or rush this stage.

I started my Podcast, Tej Talks, before I had a single property, or did a viewing. I did this because an education course which I won a free ticket to, wasn't right for me. It was taught by people who had 'been there, done that, got the t-shirt' and I was disinterested, I want relatable people doing it right now. I also needed detail, and they missed a lot.

So, what better way to document my journey and give lesser-known people the spotlight then to interview them and build my brand!

I've had 550,000+ listens in 100+ countries in 22 months and I was ranked Top 15 on the iTunes chart.

I purchased my first property in May 2019 via a Deal Sourcer, who couldn't Project Manage, overcharged and had a rubbish builder. That's another book though! I went full-time then and quit my contract. I just couldn't manage investing 150 miles from home whilst working, it can be done but it is difficult and I struggle to focus anyway, so I had to do this. I had about 14 months of savings, if not more, so I was well prepared to jump. My brand was also going strong, it really does make me happy to help people, I have no adverts or upsell on my Podcast, and the community I've built is testament to my core values; integrity, honesty, transparency, realism and passion.

In 9 months, I purchased 15 Properties, and raised £598,000 of Investor funding.

This book has the mechanics, the tricks, the tips, the lessons and much more from this experience, to help you do better than I have.

When I buy a new house, the profit or cash flow is vital, and important. But really, what drives me is the excitement and passion that I have when designing refurbishments. What tiles? What Grout? Which worktop? I love these decisions and I also enjoy bargain hunting.
My drive is not money, it's the opportunity to be creative and build a wonderful house for someone to make their home.

What I've achieved in property, you can do the same or better - I promise you. You are the only person stopping yourself.

Follow me on Instagram, that's where I share my daily woes, challenges and mistakes. With plenty of fun in between - @tej.talks

In this book, I guide you through the mechanics, the tips, tricks and smart ways of building a property portfolio. I will take you right from the beginning, to finding a property, analysing it, refurbishing it, renting and refinancing it to becoming a nice cash generating asset. I want to provide you with all the useful information and knowledge I've learnt the hard way, in an easy to digest form. I've lost money, profit and time. So, if I can save you some of that trouble, I've done a good job.

I wrote this to bridge a gap, a gap for beginners who I feel have no 'one stop shop' that covers the basics, but also the complex and more in-depth topics that aren't spoken about. I want to give you an insight into the reality of property, to show you the mistakes I've made so you can laugh and learn. I've included as much as I can without creating too much overwhelm. I share tips that I've never spoken about before, I take you through the process I have used to build my portfolio, and the efficient ways I've achieved this growth.

I will mainly be covering the BRR strategy in property, you may have heard of this before. It's a fantastic way to invest.

Tej Talks

WHAT IS BRR?

buy – refurbish – refinance

Buy Refurbish Refinance is used in many property businesses nowadays, especially when starting it out. It allows you to 'pull money out' of a deal, meaning the traditional method of a spending and leaving a 25%+ deposit in a property and then generating rental income, has evolved. This is still very common, and there's nothing wrong with it. However, with the BRR strategy you could buy four properties in one year, with the same funds as you would have used doing one. That's a lot more rent generated and a bigger asset base, who doesn't want that? It's a lot more work though, and riskier, so please don't take it as a silver bullet to success.

People look at the yield of their Buy to Let, but I think what's important is the Return On Cash Employed (ROCE) or Return On Cash Left In (ROCLI) a deal, because the purchase price or value may not be the same as your actual investment. Calculate how much money you use and keep in a property by buying the non-BRR way, then work out your return on that amount, using profit, not rent. Keep this figure to compare later in the book.

BUY

The key to this strategy is the price. Getting 5% off a property like you may get traditionally is out of the question. You need 40%+ below the end value (or GDV) of the property. This applies usually outside of London. If you're in London you could buy at near market value and add a lot of value through extensions etc., however in some parts of the UK the cost of work is more than the added value. So, we secure our profit on purchase. How do you secure property so cheap? There are a multitude of ways, of which we have an entire chapter on, for now just trust me that it is possible, I've purchased 15 so far and all have been significantly under the 'current' and end value. This stage requires a lot of Due Diligence, a level of risk and confidence - all of which I will talk through in detail. Patience is also required for BRR in this stage, you'll do a lot of viewings.

I meant *a lot*, before securing just one property. Be prepared!

There is a miseducation that you should buy using a mortgage (preferably without an ERC), do the refurb, then refinance again onto another mortgage. This is a misuse of the product, Mortgages are 25+ year term products, not 6-month loans, that's what bridging, and cash is for. Lenders will soon notice and red list you, and that's not what you want just to save a couple thousand pounds. If the deal does not stack with interest payments/bridging fees, then your margins may be too tight. Bridging - another tool we will cover together.

Buying is cash intensive, like all of the BRR stages. We'll talk through case studies of my properties, The good, The bad and the ugly. I want you to really understand the figures as they are key to this stage in particular. Buying houses can be frustratingly slow, thank Solicitors and Land Registry for that.

REFURBISH

So, you've purchased a house and got through conveyancing, signing lots of paperwork and organising finance. It gets easier now right?

Nope.

I find refurbs the most exciting and interesting stage, I love building/creating things and seeing them come to life, as well as making wonderful homes for people. Knowing you're changing your local market from Tenant/Agent feedback and seeing what others produce, is a great feeling. It takes a lot of hard work and bargain hunting to increase your margins and your buffers (these are vital).

Finding builders is a very tricky task, you will make mistakes and you're likely to lose some money along the way, especially if you don't Invest locally. This stage requires you to be the most ruthless and unforgiving in my opinion, mistakes on refurbs can be so costly to fix and poor workmanship is just embarrassing. I've had a nightmare with my first and second builders (although calling them that is offensive to the trade!) to the extent that I had a full-on mental break down from all the lies, manipulation and shocking quality of work. Plus, ongoing legal cases. I hope this book helps you avoid that situation; I've made mistakes which I'll share as learnings for you.

This stage is very important to ensure you maximise the floor space of the property, increase its value (for the next stage and to increase your rent) and fix all the issues you purchased it with. There are common things you should spend money on to ensure a good tenant experience but also low maintenance for you, which is one way to make this more 'passive'.

Most refurbishments I have done in this strategy have been £15,000+, usually a full replaster, rewire, new bathroom, kitchen, doors and more. I have achieved a BRR with a refurb of around £5,000. Why? How? I revert to the first stage - I buy at the right price to achieve my end goal. It's vital you buy at the right price, it's the main variable you can control. Refurbs will have aspects that are non-negotiable. For example, if the house has damp, you must fix this, or the electrics aren't up to standard, you must upgrade. Do not cut corners.

REFINANCE

This requires a lot of due diligence before you even buy the property, and it does take time and patience to do. There's a manual method... and yeah, that's the only method. I can't see a software yet that does this right. I'll get to this in detail later, but for now please be aware that the end value of your property is crucial to the success of the BRR model. There will always be an element of risk here, that you can factor for, but not stress about - else you'd never buy a house.

This is called a 're' finance as you are replacing the first form of finance (bridge/cash) with another, so essentially, it's the second form of finance on the house. The legal process is easier and is totally in your Solicitors control as there is no 'other side' to slow things down. However, some lenders will be total snails about this, frustratingly.

It's essential you work with a broker on this part, because there are 100s of products on the market, and you'll find that your selection may be limited because of one of many potential factors. I don't own a residential home, my salary is minimal, and I've quickly become a portfolio landlord, my portfolio has recently been in negative cash flow (quick growth). My lender pool is limited for the time being, that's okay because my broker sorts the best deals for me and does all the research (hard work).

Please, speak to a broker before you buy a deal and before you quit your job and galivant off into the sunset with a tenner in the bank. You need to ascertain how 'mortgageable' you and potential properties are.

BONUS: flips

This book is about BRR not FLIPS, however I think it's important I touch on this briefly, as it can be done alongside your main approach. It's what I do, in fact all my flip profits go to pay my Investors interest back. I wish I took the profit from it and got myself some new trousers, been years since Zara has heard from me. This is an effective (but still challenging way) of generating cash to repay Investors, or to take chunks of profit.

The process is similar to a BRR, but there is no refinance, it's a sale. The refurbishment is also slightly different, you're selling to someone so you should still ensure it's of good quality and will last long, but you're likely to spend more on design. You want someone to walk in, fall in love with it, tell the agent there and then they want to offer, above asking, to secure it. You know this feeling, right? When you eat an incredible meal, discover a great product, buy your own family home? It's natural and it's the feeling you want to create.

You don't want them to think *"Oh it's good, but we don't like XYZ"*

You want them to say, "WOW".

If you follow this guide but alter your refurb to include a higher-spec kitchen, with more design elements, and apply the same to the bathroom, making it feel higher spec by tiling floor to ceiling, as opposed to none or up to 1m. Consider a full replaster as opposed to a part-plaster, look for carpets that are more premium, fancier skirting boards and swag door handles. Chrome fittings instead of white plastic is a nice touch for flips, that doesn't cost much. Use Pinterest for inspiration and what other people are doing for flips, visit my website to see the difference in level. When it comes to selling - use an agent, buyers are such headache-inducers, and you've got better things to do.

My guide for finding a lettings agent will also somewhat serve for you to find a selling agent too. Most of the time, I will sell via the same agent that got me the house - relationships first, I want more deals!

This is not an all-encompassing guide to flips, but a small section to highlight some of the differences.

[CASE STUDY 1] – 2TIRP

Purchase Price: £70,000
Stamp Duty (SDLT): £2,100
Sourcing Fee: £2,700
Conveyancing Fee: £1,000
Refurbishment: £10,826
Interest on Finance: £3,626

Total money in: £90,837

RICS Valuation: £115,000

Remortgage Amount (75% LTV): £86,250

Money left in: £4,587*

<u>Monthly</u>
Rent: £650
Mortgage Cost: £230
Insurance Cost: £20
Cash flow/Profit: £400

Annual Cashflow/Profit: £4,281 **
ROCLI: 93%

* This means I pulled out all of my initial money in minus £4,587, so you could say that it is left in the deal, as it's the only initial money that didn't get paid back out on the remortgage. The remortgage was 75% of the end value, so £86,250 and I had spent £90,837 (costs, purchase, refurbishment, interest, everything) on the property. So, £4,587 is my

actual 'investment' over the long term. **This is after I've removed £500 for maintenance and certificates etc.

My costs were high because this was purchased from a sourcer, imagine how good it would be without the sourcing fee, as a % ROCLI.

RICS Valuation means that a RICS-qualified surveyor has assessed the property for remortgage purposes. This is usually done by the mortgage lender, so they know how much they can lend.

I highlight this example early on to show you what is achievable by anyone, this was my second ever deal and the tenants are fantastic. Thanks to Investor funds and some clever Bridging, I put £0 into this deal. The calculations and figures will make a lot more sense as you read this book.

THE GOOD & BAD

of single-let properties

POSITIVE	NEGATIVE
Little management, tenant type can be as hands-off as you can get	Each property will cash flow considerably less than an HMO or SA
Solid foundation of a portfolio provides you with 'Landlord Experience' for Lenders	You need a large number of them to produce significant cash flow
No paying of bills, council tax, TV license etc	One bad tenant could mean no income at all from that house
Maintenance should be lower than an HMO, if the refurbishment is done right	Slow strategy, can take many months to produce profit
Low entry requirements for Lenders and capital upfront	Will not allow you to quit your job quickly, it's a long-term wealth building strategy
Refurbishment is often not as capital intensive as bigger projects	Will not work in every area, it requires specific factors and figures
Always in demand, rental is strong for 'family homes' nationwide	
Risk of bad tenants is spread across multiple houses/Rental agreements	
Ability to pull out all of your initial money, and then some, allowing you to recycle your cash	

Tej Talks

MENTAL
FOUNDATIONS

start with your mind

So far, we have gone through the basics of this strategy with a brief insight into each stage. You might think we will now get stuck into the process and how you can implement it.

Not just yet.

It is absolutely vital that you build your foundations in your mindset, attitude and mentality before even viewing a property. Your mind has to be ready for the endless challenges and issues of Property, whilst being ready to survive the tough times. Also, you have to understand the balance between being critical, celebrating your victories and not getting carried away or complacent in the good times. If you read Stoicism, you'll recognise a lot of what I'm saying, and I hope it reinforces your belief, for those new to it - I recommend some books at the end of this book. I'm going to explain the mindset I think you need to be successful in property (and business) by sharing some philosophy, then explaining how this relates to investing.

"If it is not right, do not do it, if it is not true, do not say it."
– Marcus Aurelius

OPERATE WITH INTEGRITY

This is the simplest principle to understand, yet the most difficult for the world to act on. Imagine what Earth would be like if everyone followed just this one thought?

Look around you, people prove that it's easy to scam people out of money, it's straightforward to convince others that they are God's gift to the world and it's surprisingly easy to make good money from doing bad things. Does that mean you should do it? Does that mean you take the unethical shortcut just because it's easier? No.

Many people do, they always have, and they always will. The only way to act in business and in life is to be honest and operate ethically with good morals. These will change between people, but there are general principles we can agree on across cultures, languages and borders.

If you lie in this business, you will get caught out. If you behave immorally, you will get caught out.

Just don't do it, there's no reason to. Act with integrity and you will make more money in the long run. Look at the wealthiest and most inspirational people to you and assess their integrity. Your reputation is especially vital in Property, where you require people to trust you enough to loan you Private Finance. So much of this business is relationship based.

This applies to refurbishments; tenant and buyer safety is paramount, so don't take shortcuts. If you go over budget making a house safe and liveable, then that's what you must do. Remember this means less maintenance and hassle, so over the long run you'll make more money. If you're a deal sourcer, and you mislead people on end values or refurbishment costs, say goodbye to a long-term relationship that would have paid you ten times more than that one deal.

We all make mistakes though, sorry is a powerful word when you mean it and offer a solution.

"Nothing is good or bad, but thinking makes it so"
– Shakespeare

YOU DECIDE WHAT YOU SEE

This is a core stoic principle and will change your life when you implement it, it takes time but the transformation in your thinking will be incredible.

Nothing has a sentiment, everything is 'neutral'. We apply the meaning to it, we decide what it means to us, and how it makes us feel. We are in control of our perception. We decide how we take the person cutting us up on the motorway, or the comment from a friend, or the inflammatory remark a partner may make. Take a deep breath when you feel 'some type of way' and give yourself a break from the instant 'stimuli = response' that we are accustomed to, take a moment to decide how you will perceive something. That space is the moment you decide how you take something, and what your reaction is, it's a very powerful moment.

Everything has a positive or negative angle, everything. Let's look at some practical examples:

Deal falls through, seller pulls out, you lose £500 legal fees. This sounds bad right?

What if the house had structural issues you never noticed plus Knotweed that was hidden in Winter? What if the end value was not as you anticipated because the EPC was incorrect, or the market shifted? Were there clues in the seller/agent behaviour that may have hinted at them pulling out? Potentially. At the very least you've learnt a lesson here about the ease at which deals can go wrong, and perhaps you now negotiate no sale no fee terms with your Solicitor to save £500

Tej Talks

next time. Or, you complain, get angry, get annoyed at your monetary loss and affect your personal life and other business aspects. Meaning, you lose more money anyway.

You're offered 5% less than your asking price on a flip. Annoying?

It's a cash buyer, who wants to complete in 14 days. Then, you get an offer from a Mortgage buyer who will likely take 2 months, and then some. What do you do? How do you feel? This is a time to take a step back and analyse this as a business decision not a personal perception of someone trying to offer you less. Take the money, it's only 5% and if you can get out and on to another deal quicker, you'll make more money in the long term, instead of being hung up on 5%. Or, you could be angry at the world for not giving you what you wanted, for the builder for not chasing that one socket or god for not answering your prayers. You could get worked up, miss this offer, the market shifts then have to accept 20% less.

You're sent to prison. (Didn't expect this example, did you?)

This could be a perfect time to reflect on your life, away from the pressures and stimuli that normal life brings you. This is a time to read, philosophise, learn a language, learn who you really are and experience something totally new. It's a time to work on your fitness, and perhaps even your influence. Yes, it's a terrible thing, and nobody wants to go there and it's not a nice place. However, if you shift your perception to dealing with the cards you are dealt, you can make the most of them and see the 'other side' of what is generally regarded as an incredibly negative and damaging experience. Or, you see it as the end of your life, a mental imprisonment, bad luck, a place to beat yourself up and give in to the world. Somewhere you change your entire personality, lose hope in yourself and the world, then come out much worse than you went in.

"It never ceases to amaze me: we all love ourselves more than other people but care more about their opinion than our own."
– Marcus Aurelius

FOCUS ON YOUR OWN JOURNEY

With social media and networking, it's all too easy to feel envious or upset that others appear to be doing so much, earning good money and buying lots of Properties. You'll also be distracted by the plethora of strategies on offer - the infamous 'shiny penny' affects us all, and it's a normal part of this industry, I think we all need to go through it to come out stronger.

Everyone is on a different path, with their own timeframes, goals, and starting positions. Just remember that not all is what it looks like, just because someone has something you don't, it doesn't mean their life is problem free and that they are happy. After all, life is too short to be rich and unhappy? Not everyone will share the negatives and challenges, which is why I emphasise these aspects and share when things go wrong via my social media. You'll learn who is realistic after following them for a while. If you are following the right steps, with the right mindset you will achieve everything you want to, I have no doubts. If you let others' progress cloud your mind, it's only going to rain for you, so get your wellies on or focus inwards. You'll figure out whose opinions you respect over time.

This also relates to people's direct opinions of you, if you put yourself out there, especially on social media, you will attract some haters and trolls, but to be honest, not as many as you think. I've had ten in almost two years, and I'm very active. The way you should take other's

Tej Talks

opinions is as 'feedback', ignore the *way* they said something, and focus on the content. Think about it for a moment, is what they're saying true? Do you behave or come across like that? Ask someone close to you. Haters do provide great feedback; they just don't always know how to package it. If they're rude or continue to hate, just block them. I rarely reply, it's a waste of time and only adds negativity to your life. Also, they are busy hating on the internet behind a screen, and you're out here buying houses, who's winning I ask you!?

Over time your own opinion will get stronger, more accurate and you will believe in it more. At the start it is difficult when the so called 'experts' are calling you out, however, often, most people are actually just trying to help, and will be really nice. So listen carefully, as there is a lot of free knowledge out there.

"If you know not which port you sail, no wind is favourable."
– Seneca

CLEAR GOALS AND PATHWAY

I love this thought. Stop for a moment and reread it, take a deep breath and just understand what's being said. Property like most businesses can be a numbers game, what this means is you need to do X many viewings, put in X many offers and get rejected X many times from Investors before having success. If you're not set on your goals and your why, then how will you know if an opportunity or threat has presented itself?

If you don't know where you're heading, things become fuzzy and obscured. Your day to day activities will seem meaningless, because you're confused about the end goal, so why are you doing this instead of that? What's the difference? Why is this significant? These are

Tej Talks

questions you don't want to be asking, once you're clear on your vision everything else makes more sense.

I'm not suggesting you have solid, unchanging goals from day one. However, setting SMART goals from the start will be a massive help on this journey, but these are flexible and will change. We cover these in the next section.

Understanding your motivation, deeper than the Bentley(s) or holidays, really reflecting on this, will ensure that your ship is sailing to the right port, and picking up the best winds.

Internalising this philosophy and applying it to your life means you will see obstacles as challenges, things to go through and not to turn or run from. It means you will have a purpose, and as humans we really need this to be intrinsically happy, we want to feel like we matter. When you speak to people, having this clarity about 'which port you sail' will come across as confidence, and life is a lot easier with confidence.

Some days you will feel like you are drifting in the Ocean, and no winds are favourable. This is normal, especially at the start. This book will give you the tools to reduce these days and increase those full speed ahead days and ensure that you have full control. Taking action is important, even if it's small steps to move forward on those down days, just be persistent.

"If anyone can refute me, show me I'm making a mistake or looking at things from the wrong perspective, I'll gladly change. It's the truth I'm after, and the truth never harmed anyone."
– Marcus Aurelius

STRONG OPINIONS, LOOSELY HELD

You will be 'wrong' a lot, you'll not have the right knowledge, you'll think it's A when it's really B. You must reframe this, it doesn't matter if you are wrong or right, that's a construct of your ego. You either learn, or you have already learnt that lesson.

When we start out in Property, or any business we will not have all the knowledge, experience or insight, and we have to realise that, or else we will never learn. People are very helpful in property, ask, and we shall answer! There's nothing stupid about making mistakes, not knowing the answer or asking lots of questions. I mean, how else do you learn?

When asking for help, the better the question, the better the answer. Asking big broad questions is unlikely to get you anything but a broad generic answer. Give detail, ask a specific question and your response will be a lot more helpful. Trust me, a lot of people ask me questions via Social Media, and I've seen the variety of ways people ask, and I know what I respond better to.

The world is evolving, you should be too. Accept feedback, accept when someone refutes you (with good evidence or explanation of course), reflect on it and implement a change. Some people will offer their 'corrections' in a tactless way, especially on the internet, ignore the way they've said it and look for the useful aspect of what they have said. You aren't here to be wrong or right or to have the upper hand, you're here to learn and be a good person.

> *"I judge you unfortunate because you have never lived through misfortune. You have passed through life without an opponent—no one can ever know what you are capable of, not even you."*
> *– Seneca*

EMBRACE CHALLENGES

If life was easy, we'd be bored. You, as an Entrepreneur know this, we love creating and growing businesses. Look at the Silicon Valley Mil/billionaires, they don't retire at 26, they take that money and start again, and invest, they become part of the start-up ecosystem again. We can't stop, it's a curse... and a blessing! Learn to love the process.

Property is going to slap you, right across the face, then a backhand, or three. Then it will punch you in the gut and push you over in the mud. Not once - but often. That's the reality, you are going to face so many challenges, you need resilience to make it here. Real mental grit.

People will let you down, lie, cost you money, damage your health, slow you down and quite frankly, annoy you. Refurbishments will go over budget, over time and cause a domino effect of issues. Solicitors will complain and be slow, brokers will introduce you to the wrong deals and lenders will pull out the day before completion. Investors will waste your time consistently, claim they are going to invest, then disappear or make excuses. People will belittle you, be negative about your journey, criticise you, make stupid comments online and not trust you. I could go on. But I hope this explains the reality. If these challenges excite you - you're as weird as me!

Tej Talks

If you haven't seen darkness, then you don't know light. Makes sense, right? If you don't know challenges, then the good times aren't that good, it's just normal. If you haven't made mistakes, then how do you deal with the next mistake? How do you know your potential? We are limitless, but you don't know what you could achieve unless you push the boundary and embrace challenges. Also, the more scars you have, the more Investable you are. Would you feel safer giving your money to someone who has experience and has lived through the issues of a Property business, or someone who will be handling it for the very first time?

"I begin to speak only when I'm certain what I'll say isn't better left unsaid." – Cato

CURB YOUR EGO

Ego, as Ryan Holliday aptly puts it, is "An unhealthy belief in our own importance. Arrogance. Self-centred ambition."

Have you noticed I don't really share my opinion on stuff? I just don't care about certain things and I also know that it's very easy to get caught up in a fight of opinions on the internet, get emotionally involved and carry a lot of angst and anger at the world. During the COVID19 Pandemic, Facebook transformed into a plethora of posts on every single element of it, with many expert Virologists, Epidemiologists and Politicians (*doesn't take much, just be a good liar?!*) coming out of the woodwork. I didn't comment on anything, because frankly it's better left unsaid. I also had a call from 2 tradesmen having a heated fight, and I could have easily told them they are being childish, stupid and to curb their egos. That was better left unsaid, I became very objective and handled it from a distance, using humour. Despite the fact I thought it was ridiculous.

Sometimes, we don't need to comment, even when we feel slighted, belittled or confused, internal reflection and dialogue can be the best remedy. I'm not saying don't stand up for yourself but pick your battles and think about what leaves your mouth. Prevention is better than cure, which means; not creating an issue is a lot easier than fixing one.

Many times, I have said things that I shouldn't have, it's cost me relationships and money, I've learnt the hard way. Take a deep breath, separate the stimuli from the response, that little gap will make life so much easier. It's a simple technique with deep effects when used consistently - pause more often and let your mind catch up with reality.

To summarise:
- Curb your ego
- Embrace challenges
- Strong opinions, loosely held
- Clear goals and pathway
- Focus on your own journey
- You decide what you see
- Operate with integrity

Before I show you how to build your Property Business, I have to share the reality of what you're about to embark on. Most adverts online and training companies will make property seem a lot easier than it is. Let's cut the crap and I'll show you what to *really* expect.

Every element of Property will take longer than expected, often for no reason.

Every refurbishment will go over the initial budget and timeframe.

Every project will bring up new types of issues with a building, every single time.

You will likely view 50 houses, offer on 40, to have 1 accepted.

You will likely engage with 50 people, before you get 1 that actually invests money with you.

You will go to 10 networking events in a row and raise no money.

You'll bid on 15 properties and maybe win 1, if you keep emotional control.

You will piss people off, and end relationships that could have been beneficial.

Your first Podcast, FB post, Video, Blog etc. will be total crap with minimal engagement. It takes time, don't give up right away.

You will have more rejections than you've ever had, agents will laugh in your face.

Sellers will pull out last minute, tenants will damage your house and not pay rent.

Pipes will burst, boilers will break, and roofs will need repair. When you least expect it.

Builders will rip you off, short-change you and lie. They will act lovely and caring, then stab you in the back and cost you a lot of money.

You'll be strapped for cash one week, then very liquid the next.

Solicitors may make mistakes that can be costly.

Brokers will mislead you to pick a product that pays them well, or just lack sufficient knowledge.

You may feel lonely, no matter how many events you go to or JVs you have, this can affect us all.

Utility companies will send your blood pressure through the roof.

Some days, everything will fall apart.

Some days, you will be so tired mentally and physically you'll never want to see Rightmove again.

People will drive you up the wall, they will lie, cheat, act irrationally and be totally ridiculous.

People will ask the most broad, unhelpful (to themselves) questions and expect a specific and useful answer, also known as ASKHOLES.

If that's put you off investing in Property yourself, then put the book down, give me a call and you can invest with me. Just kidding! Sort of.

Seriously though, it isn't for everyone and that is not a problem.

Do what you love, life is too short.

Despite this, you are building wealth and assets for life, and generations after you. This will provide the most 'passive' form of income you can generate as far as I know. It is incredibly rewarding, when it goes well, when all the pieces fit together and your vision comes to life - you'll forget everything I just said, and want to do it again, and again.

GOAL SETTING

start with the end

Firstly, it is very important to understand your why. This is personal to you; it doesn't matter what anyone else thinks or what their reasons are. Why are you in property? Ask yourself this, what do you want to achieve? What drives you? Are you doing this for yourself, or your family? Do you actually want to do this? Why is it important you succeed? I suggest watching a TED talk by Simon Sinek on 'Start with Why'.

This is an important step and one that requires some reflection and time alone for you to process this. When times get tough, and you feel like giving up, and even in the good times when you're searching for meaning - your why will be right by your side to keep you going. Believe me, you will need it and you will be so grateful you carried out this exercise.

All goals should follow this general principle:

S - Specific
M - Measurable
A - Achievable
R - Realistic
T - Time bound

Goal setting can be done in a variety of ways, I'll take you through the method I teach and how I implement the SMART approach *(first implemented in 1981 by George T. Duran).*

Let's start with your sexy goals. This means the life you want to live, the dream house, marble worktop, supercars, clothes, cosmetics, travelling the world, raising a family, living in your favourite place, having a holiday home, donating to charity, no financial worries and whatever else makes you smile and deeply satisfied. Write this down,

Tej Talks

create a vision board with images of it, have it somewhere that you will see often. Close your eyes and imagine how your future life will feel. Don't worry about what others want, or are ambitious for, this is your future so it can be as big or small, frugal or extravagant as you want. Think about what you want in order to live your best life.

Now you know the ultimate goal that you are aiming for, let's plan your monetary goals. How much will your future life cost you per month? Break down each item carefully, research how much certain things cost, and build up a spreadsheet of what your monthly outgoings are likely to be, any one-off costs you can split monthly for the sake of keeping this exercise clear. I've given an example below, just to demonstrate how you could do this. It's not comprehensive but it shows you how yours may look. Add everything on here, every little detail and cost you may have.

Mortgage	£2,000
Groceries (Waitrose darling, of course)	£500
Car (Yellow Lamborghini?)	£1,200
Skincare (yes, this is a priority!)	£150
Surplus/Investing	£2,000
Pets (got to feed the fish)	£100
Family	£200
TOTAL PER MONTH	**£6,150**

Tej Talks

Don't forget the basics like Mortgage, bills, food, insurance, maintenance, eating out and all that fun stuff. If you want to add 'taking Tej to Nandos' in there, go for it!

You should now have a monthly figure, I'm going to use £10,000 per month as an example, it's also the most common amount I hear. £10,000 a month is the figure you are looking for pre-tax, I'm not going to discuss tax because we will all pay different amounts depending on our company structures, accountants, decisions on withdrawing money, other directors in a company etc.

£10,000 per month in income is equal to £120,000 a year pre-tax. So, how do you go about generating this? We will go off the conservative assumption that each BTL you purchase will cashflow (profit) £250 per month. This is after mortgage, management and maintenance, more details on this later. *(In reality, my BTLs generate close to £325, but we are using worst-case).*

Every 4 BTLs will generate £1,000 per month.

So, you need £10,000/£250 = 40 BTLs.

I told you this was the slow and long way to build cash flow - the math shows it. Compare that to HMOs where you'd need 8-10 of them, producing £1,000-£1,250 each in profit. If you stop reading now and want to buy HMOs, then I don't blame you. They are attractive but refer to the pros/cons list we went through earlier.

So, the target is 40 BTLs. How long could this take? I purchased 12 BTLs in 9 months (*+3 flips*), if Coronavirus hadn't hit the UK, I predict this would become 17 BTLs after 12 months being a full-time property investor, this would generate £4,250 according to our sums so far.

I think it then seems fair, following that I personally could buy another 23 the next year. So that's 40 over 2 years and £10,000 cash flow. However, from what I can see this isn't the norm. I also spent 6 months prior networking, learning, podcasting and building my brand. My brand has made a lot of this possible, if you're choosing not to create one or take it seriously then it's hard to compare.

I suggest that 40 BTLs over 3 years is realistic, but difficult. I suggest you challenge yourself to 2.5 years in this example. But, please note this is all an example to show you the process of setting this. It doesn't matter what my numbers are compared to yours, we are all on our own paths. However, people always ask what's realistic especially compared to popular trainers/educators, so I'm sharing this.

Now this next part can be difficult to take in, and it may feel unsurmountable, but this book, my podcasts and eLearning are here to guide you.

So, 40 Buy to Lets. Let's say you're purchasing with bridging loans, mortgages or investors who give you 75% of the purchase price. This % is called the Loan to Value, most institutional lenders will loan up to 75% of the property value as a rule of thumb, so you have to fund the 25% of the purchase price. This is the deposit requirement when using most finance methods.

Let's assume you're buying in an area like Yorkshire or Liverpool where the BRR model works really well. I will make the example purchase price £100,000, to keep the maths simple.

You need 25% of £100,000 to buy one house. That's £25,000.

So, 40 BTLs means you need 25% of (£100,000 x 40) = £1,000,000.

You need £1 million in deposits to reach your goal, over 3 years. This sounds big. Wait, it gets bigger;

There is of course Stamp Duty Land Tax (SDLT) and Legal Fees to be paid at the very minimum, so we can add 3% for SDLT and then say 1% for legals, that's an extra 4%.

So, in reality to get the keys to the houses:

40 BTLs means you need 29% of (£100,000 x 40) = £1,160,000.

Not too much of an increase proportionately.

However, this isn't all you need to carry out a BRR. You've just got the keys now, which is fantastic, but you need funds for the refurbishment. You have to add value to the house now, in order to get a suitable refinance and recycle your cash.

Let's say you need £20,000 to refurb each house. Being conservative here. That's 20% of purchase, so add that to what we have currently which sits at 29%, and then you need 49% of purchase price, to Buy, Refurbish and get the house to a stage where you can Refinance, and go again.

Let's run the maths again:

40 BTLs means you need 49% of (£100,000 x 40) = £1,960,000.

Shit just got real.

Let's not worry about where you will find this from, or whatever your personal amount is, that comes later. However, we now have a goal for how much finance we need to have, agreed?

So far, our goals are Specific; 40 BTLs generating £10,000 per month (conservatively), whilst raising £1,960,000 to purchase the properties. They are Measurable, because it is very straightforward to track these figures accurately. They are achievable and also Realistic; however, they are not easy, this will be very challenging. Time-bound is covered too because we've agreed on 3 years as a timeframe. The goals we have talked about fit within with the SMART method. You can now break these down into quarterly/monthly/daily Key Performance Indicators (KPIs) to suit you, and these small activities will compound and equate to achieving your big end goal.

Your goals may change over time, you may realise they were too big or too small, you may take a totally different path, or even stop buying properties and loan your funds out instead, who knows. Your goals must be flexible and as you evolve as a person, they will too.

Write down your goals, perhaps in a spreadsheet so you can track them and reward yourself at intervals. I also like turning cells green when I've achieved that goal, it's pretty rewarding and free!

Right, that was a lot of maths and talking through some concepts we haven't got into yet, so if you want to continue reading and come back, please do.

COMPANY FOUNDATIONS

start as you mean to go on

SETTING UP YOUR COMPANY

Speak to a Property Accountant about what would suit your personal situation first.

If you are going to buy more than a few properties, it may be best to do so via a Ltd. company. You may hear this referred to as an 'SPV' or Special Purpose Vehicle. This is used when you set up a Ltd company for a special use, such as holding an asset with you and a JV partner etc. Different from the past where you'd likely buy in your personal name, Section 24 of the Finance Act means the profit in that scenario has decreased for reasons I won't cover.

By purchasing in a Ltd. Company, it also means you have a more tax efficient vehicle to withdraw money from and operate a clean separation from your personal tax affairs.

Think of the Ltd. company as a 'wrapper', you are not the company, but you will own 100% of it, but it is a separate entity. Also, you will barely benefit from the 'limited liability' or protection that comes from a company, as any Bridgers or Mortgage Lenders will make you sign personal guarantees anyway. We'll cover that later, as it's pretty serious.

Check the table below for a comparison from my Accountant at the time of writing. *This is not professional advice.*

	SOLE TRADER	LIMITED COMPANY
Section 24 tax relief	Mortgage interest restricted for higher rate taxpayers	Mortgage interest is allowable in full
Mortgage interest	Often lower than limited company	Higher than sole trader
Profit extraction	Taxed on profits, regardless of what's drawn out	Shareholders control salary & dividends, which can be very tax efficient. Can bring family members in and benefits for inheritance tax planning.
Tax	Depends on your current rate	Lower overall if planned effectively
Capital Gains Tax (CGT)	Payable on gain within 30 days of sale	No CGT, but corporation tax with a longer payment period.
Accountancy fees	Cheaper	More expensive

You may need two separate Ltd companies for flips and BTLs, to separate the heavily financed (mortgaged) company from the one that will have a higher throughput of property. In addition, if something goes wrong with a flip, you want it separate from your other assets, for

Tej Talks

your own protection. Having a group structure, allows you to transfer properties between companies in case you have to refinance one in your flip company, i.e. if it doesn't sell or you change your mind. It also means you can offset losses in one company against the other, but I'll let the professionals explain this further. Please seek professional help.

I won't talk you through setting this up, there are lots of guides online. However, getting your SIC code(s) correct is important, so I've listed these below. Always speak to a professional, I am not giving legal advice.

68100 - Buying and selling of own real estate - for FLIPS

68209 - Other letting and operating of own or leased real estate - for BTLs

If you are setting up a JV company as your main vehicle of Investment, then you can allocate shares accordingly in the set up. Please, make sure you have a solid JV or Shareholders agreement written by a professional. If you are holding properties together this is even more important, you need to agree and be bound by certain conditions and 'what-ifs'. Believe me, even with the best intentions, the best of relationships can turn sour real quick, especially when money is involved.

When it comes to choosing a name for your main Ltd company and if you're going to focus on building a company brand, then it is useful for the registered name to be the same as the one you will market. However, you can still have a trading name that is different from your registered one. For example: "Property Investment Ltd" is your name at Companies House, but you trade under "We Love Yellow Properties" on your marketing and materials.

BANK ACCOUNTS

There are a number of bank accounts to choose from. Research is key. The following are things to look out for:

- A long period without charges (or very minimal charges)
- How established they are
- How your money is protected
- What their support/staff are like
- If they are comfortable handling large transactions
- Account spending or storage limits
- Integration with accounting software
- Any other particular features you may need

I use Tide for my holding (main) company, and Starling for my flip company. Starling is quick, has partial statements so you can get proof of funds instantly, and great support. However, I find the interface unclear and not as easy to glance at as Tide. Tide has a great interface and categories, so it's efficient to use. They do have small limits, so increase these as soon as you open the account. I'm trying to use Monzo business because I think Monzo are awesome, but at the time of writing they don't do Business accounts to companies that generate income from assets (rental income). I've had Santander and HSBC before, no complaints, but their apps and interfaces are not as slick as the challenger banks, plus, I prefer start-ups. Also, they haven't got the 'interesting' history some of these old banks have...

SYSTEM SET UP

Project Management Tools

Using a Project Management tool is very useful, I used to use a combination of my spreadsheets and my whiteboard, it became impossible. I use Asana which gives a very clear view of where projects are and allow multiple collaborators. You may want to use these purely for refurbishments, or to track the whole process from offer to completion, refurbishment, refinance and to letting it out. Experiment and see what work for you, there are many options out there like Trello or Monday. Staying in control is vital.

To do list
The most basic but useful tool you can have. Don't have a to-do list that gets bigger every day, I've done that and it's so damaging for your mental health and sense of achievement, it gets overwhelming. Have two categories, one 'master list' that has everything you need to do, and gets added to when you think of something, but then have a 'today' list which you add the 3-5 most important tasks to, and you have to tick them off before you finish the day. Some tasks may take longer and require moving back to the Master, then back into Today when it's time.

This way, you have achieved something every day, and it's so satisfying to tick through things. I use 'Microsoft To Do'. You could even block your calendar out under the headings of each task, and that functions like your 'Today' list - whatever works for you.

Contact Management (CRM system)
When you meet someone, what do you do with their details or business cards? Consider using a CRM system, there are a few free ones, I quite like HubSpot. Add everyone to this and it allows you to follow up with emails or calls at a later date and keeps things organised. This is a lot of admin work, you could find a Virtual Assistant who you send pictures of business cards to, and they can add it in. Relationships are built in the follow up.

Spreadsheets (Set up on day 1):

- Deal analysis sheet (create your own or use mine, refine this with real examples and see how it performs and how you react to it)
- Viewing tracker to ensure you follow up and stay abreast of your progress (this could be on a CRM system, but I find sheets clearer, you want address, last engaged day, most recent offer, agent name and a link)
- Assets & Liabilities (A table showing your Properties, Purchase price, End value, mortgage amount, date purchased, address, rental, monthly cash flow, Tenure, Lender names as a minimum) I have a ready-made template with formulae I can share with you if you email me with proof you've left a book review on Amazon.
- Property Cost Trackers for each deal (Refurb cost, progress, invoices paid, actual vs budget, material costs) this is vital for staying on budget and analysing how you can cut costs
- Materials list (build a sheet of your favourite taps, worktops, kitchens, toilets, tiles etc. so you can quickly build each refurb's design out)
- Cash flow projections (how your portfolio will look for the next 6-12 months with current and expected purchases, and when you think each will start to cash flow)

Cloud based file storage:

- Store all your spreadsheets here so they are accessible anywhere and can be shared easily
- Store your proof of ID, Address and Funds here ready to send to Agents or Solicitors
- Create folders for every property and store before/after pictures

- Use folders to organise legal documents, ASTs, Gas Certificates, Electric Certificates and others that will all build up over time
- I use Google Drive, but Dropbox and OneDrive amongst others are available.

Finance:
- Set up a bookkeeping software and automate it, you can create rules, so you don't have to manually assign your transactions
- Quickbooks (I use), Xero and FreeAgent are the most popular Bookkeeping platforms

A lot of this stuff won't be used until you are actively buying but build the foundations strong so as you get busier this is ready for you. Then you don't have to think about the admin or finding documents in a mess.

BRAND SET UP

This is a very light introduction to this; I could write an entire book on Branding!

Email

Don't even think about having a free gmail. No. Stop right there, go to 1&1/GoDaddy/Google and get a custom domain, from day one. I shed a tear every time I see a @gmail on a business card, it looks so amateur. You are a business professional who should be taken seriously, so spend the £2 a month and look the part. Using admin@ or postmaster@ is not fun, consider yourname@, hello@, hola@, hey@, hi@, info@ - be creative and memorable. On the phone to agents too, make it as simple as possible, don' make the domain too long and wordy, it's going to be annoying to spell and give out to people i.e. @propertyinvestmentcompanyinyorkshireltd.com. Be sensible!

Website

Secure a domain name early, and when you do this you may even get a custom domain email for free from the provider. This doesn't have to be much at the start, perhaps a landing page, or just a few pages. These would be useful: Home Page, About Me, Social Links, a Blog and a contact us page. I suggest Squarespace, it has very pretty templates, and it's rather restrictive, meaning no matter how bad you may be at design, they will keep it looking good. It is inexpensive too. Wix is another option, but it's very unrestricted, it may be too much for a simple property site, but if you're great at design then you'll love it. There is also WordPress, but I find it clunky.

Logo

Rooftops? Boring. Everyone does it. Spend some time on this, engage a logo designer, play around with Canva, get a pen and paper, be creative. Don't use a Vistaprint standard logo or anything like that, if you can access it so can thousands of other people. Do something unique, don't get hung up on this for weeks, but just remember this is important so give it the appropriate time it deserves. Fiverr has some great options too, much cheaper than UK based designers, but they often lack uniqueness. Pick a colour that matches your personality

Social Media

Facebook is powerful for knowledge sharing, inspiration and building yourself a brand. It has a very busy and popular Property community on it. There are lots of groups, join them all at the start and engage with people's posts. Soon you'll learn which are good, bad and the few that are toxic. Facebook also allows a wide range of Media to be shared and is a great balance between personal and business content, meaning a deeper emotional connection than say LinkedIn, which can be a bit stuffy. Despite every new social media King & Queen proclaiming LinkedIn is the best platform, there is no single winner for me.

Instagram is great for the positivity and love shared in the community, I don't think I've ever seen people hating on the 'gram, which is quite refreshing. It's also very visual, which means if you don't enjoy writing then you can still communicate effectively via videos and images. It also allows scheduling via third-party apps/tools, which means it is a platform that is less time consuming. However, Instagram stories do need consistent attention, as does using DMs and responding to comments. Hashtags can be a powerful way of expanding your reach and getting your content in front of new potential followers. If you follow the right people, it will be less of a distraction and more of a focussed business activity.

LinkedIn is great for finding Investors, and posting content that is more 'professional', it's not the nicest platform to use and navigate, but what do you expect from Microsoft? People there are interested in business, so it can create quite direct and efficient conversations. I find it less useful for learning and having a community, this may change by the time you read this.

TikTok is fairly new at the time of writing, I tried a few videos but really lacked the motivation. I think the level of talent there is amazing, and the organic reach and growth is incredible. It is evolving quickly, so when you read this, I may be a TikTok superstar - who knows!

I don't use Twitter apart from complaining to companies, most respond quickly there.

NETWORKING

This has been a big part of my success, digitally (online) and physically. You will hear everyone say, 'your network is your net worth' and you'll think it's another one of these property clichés. Until you feel the power of the people in your circle, you won't realise how true that statement is. I want to talk you through some of the plans you should put in place, and the benefits that will come from adhering to a networking schedule. To be honest, I've been pretty lazy with physical networking because the reach from social media is so powerful, but every time I go, I always learn something new, meet someone interesting and catch up with friends.

Property can be lonely, especially when you don't have a business partner, so networking is a great way to meet new people and socialise... and leave the house!

I suggest you look up all the events local to you, and your investment area if it differs, and attend them all. At the start, go all out because you want to see which ones you prefer, where the atmosphere is good, the speaker is strong and the upsell is tolerable. After a few visits, you'll know which ones to cut, and which you'll become regulars at. There's a real range, from big chain formals to smaller more casual events in differing locations. Once you've chosen events you like the most, add them in your diary and go every month without fail. I would suggest going all out, to 2 events a week when you start. However, most will cost money so please factor that in, you need to be extracting value from these events. If you budget for less, but learn more, then that's a pretty good compromise.

Networking can be daunting, walking into a room full of strangers, most people already engaged in conversation. What do you do? Who do you speak to? What if they're rude? What if you don't know anything? Argh! I can feel the anxiety just writing this. I'm a very confident person, but when I started out networking was so much scarier in my head, then in reality. Like most of our issues. I used to talk it up, and get worried about X Y Z happening, when what actually happened was, I enjoyed it, learnt lots and created relationships.

My networking top tips:
- Smile, make eye contact, stand with good posture and have a firm handshake
- Don't be afraid to introduce yourself to anyone and have fun!
- Prepare an elevator pitch (a short introduction to who you are and what you do)
- If the hosts allow people to introduce themselves to the group, take this opportunity
- Introduce yourself to the host, they may then introduce you to other people
- If there is a group speaking and you want to talk to them, just say 'sorry to interrupt, mind if I join you?'
- Prepare some standard questions that you can ask people, that will lead to further conversation such as 'what brings you here', 'how long have you been in property for', 'what's your strategy', 'how did you start', 'what do you think about X news or market change'
- Business cards are still useful, even with social media
- Aim to speak to multiple people, see this as the initial meeting where you can take contact details and follow up later for a more in-depth chat
- Listen more than you speak, but don't be afraid to share your value even if you're new, you still know something that someone else doesn't
- Take pictures - good opportunity to document content for the brand

Tej Talks

YOUR SQUAD

people over profits

The people you surround yourself with, will have a huge impact on your success. Not just your friends, family and close network, but also the professionals you work with. Take time to find the right people, you can use my recommendations who have worked with me across multiple deals or search for your own. You may need a Solicitor for bridging or Mortgages (lender dependant) to be local to you, but otherwise location shouldn't matter. Let's talk about the key players:

Solicitors and Conveyancers

Solicitors are SRA regulated, and Conveyancers are usually regulated by other bodies. With Bridging finance, they will usually require at least 1 SRA partner and that you use a Solicitor, specifically. They are more expensive, and it's the same with most remortgages. If you are buying with cash, then Conveyancers do the same job but are way cheaper, same with writing contracts. I recommend having one of each and using them appropriately.

For non-cash purchases, I suggest choosing a firm with at least 2 SRA Partners. This opens up the potential lenders, as some can be quite specific. Sometimes, Lenders will have their own approved Solicitor panel that you must choose from.

Firstly, look for recommendations, from people who have actually used them before, on multiple deals, not just someone who has an affiliate with them. You want a proven track record from someone you trust. When you speak to the solicitor, you want to feel like the conversation isn't rushed, they aren't patronising you and they communicate very clearly. I prefer working with firms that solely deal with property or have a specific property department. If a company is mentioned a lot in groups and on social media, this is a good sign. Ask them how long their average completion takes? How many 14- or 28-day completions have they done? How often do they do auction purchases? Can you have their direct number? Will they reply to emails same day? How many active cases do they have at one time? Have they worked with your chosen Lender before?

Find your legal team before your first deal, you don't want to be rushing around after an offer is accepted. You want your Solicitors details ready when you offer.

Finance Broker

For purchasing with bridging, mortgages and remortgages. They will find you the best deals out of hundreds of possible combinations and lenders, plus most mortgage lenders won't accept direct applicants. I know I'm 'cost-efficient' or as some like to say, 'cheap', but this is a cost that could make a huge difference to your deals. The right finance means you save and make more money, and deals happen smoother and quicker.

You'll find that everyone and their uncle is a mortgage broker, who claims to cover 'all of the market' and is unique. The marketing in this sector is tired, which does make those with a personal brand stand out, and that's my first point. Aim to find someone who is active online, sharing value for free and posting good content, often they are passionate about what they do. As usual, recommendations come in very useful, from people who have actually used them, vet the referrer too, who's to say they aren't lying?

You want a broker who understands your long-term goals, who provides product comparisons, who presents you with options, is open to discussion, takes the initiative, has good lender relationships, understands investing in property and is contactable. Diligence is important, they need to understand your entire lending profile; your savings, income, experience etc. to give you accurate information.

Tej Talks

Also, ask them how much the lender they are recommending pays them, you want them to be working for you, not what's best for their pocket.

Insurance Broker
To ensure your Investments are protected at the right level. It's easy to go online and get a very cheap quote for landlord or property insurance, try it. However, these don't provide the same level of protection as you may get through a broker, always compare and shop around. A broker should get you the best deal. I've not found much price difference between brokers, but the service does differ. You want someone you just email an address to, and the insurance is sorted and in place, and covers everything it should.

As usual, go off recommendations using the method I've given before, or use my broker.

Bridging Company
I know I've said earlier that a broker can sort all your Finance for you, and they can, but I prefer going direct to bridgers, a broker fee can be an unnecessary extra when dealing with lower-priced BTLs and can become a middle person that can slow it down. I like to be dealing directly with the funder, especially when using bridging on a BTL purchase that is very straightforward. Bridging is useful for buying houses as it allows you to act like a cash buyer which is less hassle, quicker and means you can purchase unmortgageable properties. It's a great way to leverage your cash to purchase more properties or more expensive ones at the same time.

Finding a good bridging company will be reliant on price, alongside the relationship, ease of use and the speed that they act. Shop around, speak to as many as you can and I think you'll find two groups, one is very expensive and more independent, then you'll find larger ones that are cheaper. I work with Together Finance, they have been easy to work with and very quick, bar our first few issues.

I think when you use a lender for the first time you will have issues, whether it's last minute requirements, additional costs, not understanding the terms or bad communication - but it gets easier, so don't lose faith.

You want to know what their repossession or default rate is, who their funders are (banks or wealthy folk), their actual (not headline) rates, usual term lengths, entry, exit fees, highest LTV they go to, if they offer refurbishment loans and how interest is paid (monthly or rolled up or deducted).

Accountant

You will be spending lots of money, and then making even more money - you want to protect this from unnecessary tax and losses, that could be avoided with the right knowledge. A good accountant can advise on the best company structure for you, as discussed before. It would be useful to engage an accountant for brief advice on company formation in line with your goals, but after this I feel they come into use nearer to your year-end. But they can advise on your bookkeeping and any actions you should take before your accounting year ends. There are a few familiar faces in property, and I would suggest using a property-specific accountant, when you have a choice why not use the specialist?

I automate my booking keeping using QuickBooks (others are available), I may engage a VA at some point. With software like this you can set rules and it will happen automatically in the background.

Ask them how many accounts they look after, how many staff they have, the average portfolio size they work on, their years of experience, how long they usually take to create accounts, and if they will be on call every so often for advice. I like to ask some random questions like what are the best ways to reduce your corporation tax return in property? Best way to draw funds out of the company? Check if the cost goes up with each property, it could get expensive.

Again, recommendations and referrals work well here, ask to speak to some of their clients for testimonials. I like Accountants who Invest themselves, as there is a deeper level of understanding when you are talking through things, and they can combine their personal and professional experience.

Builders/Tradespeople
Key to the success of the BRR and the ones who are doing the physical refurbishments, these relationships need to be tight, as they will give you the most hassle. I'll cover this in a bigger section later.

Agents
For finding your tenants, managing your portfolio and selling your flips. I will go through this in detail in later chapters.

NRLA
Very useful source of documents, advice and legal insight in the world of Investment and being a property owner. If you self-manage then it's even more useful, use code [WHW-000] for a discount, it's so cheap this is a no brainer to join. They have helped me out, with very quick response times.

These are the key players I've identified; however, the suppliers of your materials are also important for example, but often your builder will have strong local relationships. But I buy all my kitchens and swag items myself, so I build these relationships, and they do pay off in price and service.

I like a bargain, we all do. What I really like though, is efficient and proactive service. Do not always go for the cheapest option, you want the person to feel valued and to work their hardest for you. If something is too cheap or too expensive, question it. Compare prices and understand what you are getting for the money, especially with solicitors and builders, the cheapest ones somehow cost ten times more in the long run, in many ways.

DEAL ANALYSIS

spreadsheets, data and research

Before I talk you through the stages of completing a successful BRR, I must tell you what makes a great deal, and what this looks like in numbers. Now, I'm writing this book to help as many people as possible, so what works for me may not be good enough or may be overly strict by your standards. Have a play around on my spreadsheet, and see what looks attractive to you, you need to set yourself a minimum return, that you will not dip below. No emotions, just a number, keep it objective and make decision making easier. Remember, you're not living here, so put the Marble toilet seat to the side!

[CASE STUDY 2] – 2OUPS

My favourite deal to date, and the most gorgeous interior. This was meant to be a flip, which explains why it looks better than a normal BTL, even if the budget was modest. This was completed in 3 months and 3 days, which is incredible. It means I picked the keys up on day 1, and 3 months 3 days later I had the bridge and Investor paid back, and remortgage funds in my account, and a tenant secured. I recycled my cash that quickly and was ready to go again or treat my investor to a very early loan payback.

This was a 2-bed end terrace off a main street, on a side lane. The refurbishment was straightforward, apart from us finding more damp than expected due to it being high up and the end wall exposed to the weather. It hadn't been touched in years, it required a new kitchen, bathroom, boiler, rewire, damp protection, re-plaster throughout, paint/decoration, chimney flashing renewing and a few new windows.

Purchase Price: £73,000
Stamp Duty (SDLT): £2,190
Conveyancing Fee: £950
Refurbishment: £18,800
Interest on Finance: £1,226

Total money in: £96,858

RICS Valuation: £125,000

Remortgage Amount (75% LTV): £93,750

Money left in: £3,102

Monthly
Rent: £600
Mortgage Cost: £254
Insurance Cost: £22
Cash flow/Profit: £324pm

Annual Cashflow/Profit: £3,388
ROCLI*: 110%

Return On Cash Left In: This is the profit or cash flow from the property annually, compared to the money 'left in' a deal after refinance. We go through this in detail in this chapter.

Would you be happy with this deal? Your investment of £3,102 is generating £3,388 per year, before voids and tax. Ideally there shouldn't be any voids if you have a solid long staying tenant, and if you've done the refurbishment to a high standard, maintenance should

Tej Talks

be minimal. I usually take off about £500 a year for maintenance and certificates.

How many of these do you need to quit your job?

So, what makes this a great deal to me?
- Leaving £5,000 or less in the deal
- A ROCLI of 50% or more
- The speed of the entire deal

BONUS: Capital Appreciation

BEFORE PHOTOS

AFTER PHOTOS

Tej Talks

What is a deal?

What I look for in deals numerically is as simple as those 3 points, however number 3 can't be controlled until you have the offer accepted. Even then, if the seller is slow with their legal process, no matter how hard you chase, it can still be out of your control. The refurbishment and revaluation are what you can control to an extent. These are my personal requirements, yours can of course be different and will be dependent on your goals.

I put capital appreciation as a bonus, most places I invest will have this but at a much slower rate than this case study, due to the economical and geographical factors that exist in that location. I'm focussed on cash flow, because after a year or so my money left in, becomes £0, through the rent. So, growth is great but I'm only really trying to generate monthly 'passive' income. I don't specifically look for capital appreciation, however it is always welcome!

How do you put all the elements of a deal together, to provide you with these figures to compare and understand if this is a good deal?

Start at the end, what is the 'Done Up Value', what is it worth when it's fully refurbished and at its sauciest. What would a valuer tell a mortgage company this house is worth, or what would an agent sell it for, if it's a Flip. This is a very important step, even small variations here can have a big impact on your ROCLI and profit.

I use Rightmove SOLD data to understand potential End Values, Zoopla and a few other sites also have this data, but I find their interfaces clunky.

Finding end values is best done like a Surveyor would

- Preferably you need sold data from the last 6 months
- Closer the better, but up to 2 miles
- Comparable condition
- Comparable type (terraced/detached etc.)
- Comparable size (square meterage)

This can be the trickiest research to do, because of a lack of clear data or the dinosaurs at Land Registry taking months to update sales online, but I promise you this is ABSOLUTELY VITAL to your success in BRR.

There are lots of websites to find End Value data, however I find nothing beats good old Rightmove Sold Data.

Remember, this data can be a bit outdated, and the revaluation won't be done on the same day you do the research (pre-offer). It will be a few months later when the revaluation is done. So, I do a bit more work to support the end value. I check SOLD STC listings, to see what has been sold recently but not completed legally. Unfortunately, you won't get to see the sold price, but you do see what it listed for, so it helps somewhat.

Next I look at the listed price on houses for sale, to see if there has been any growth or decline in prices. Again, this is a general indicator to help me build up a big picture. Lastly, if I'm not confident I will speak to a local agent that I trust, to get their view, often I find them quite accurate - opposite to what most people think of Estate Agents inflating the price, but still, be weary.

After a while, you will learn your investment area and you'll roughly know end values in each area, although these can vary street to street, you will become very proficient in knowing these without as much research.

So, you've discovered the end value of a house you want to view, what's next?

The refurbishment is a big step in understanding a potential deal, this combined with the end value will allow you to work out profits, cash flow and what price you can offer to buy the house. We will cover this in detail later on, for your understanding in this section, I'll use an example refurb cost (shown later).

Next is the costs of purchasing, this is usually Stamp Duty Land Tax, Legal Fees and any Survey costs you may have. Do not forget these, they will soon become standard fees on every purchase when working out overall costs and profits.

Now we know the end value, the refurbishment, and buying costs, we have all we need in the formula to work out what we can buy the property at.

Now you know the formula, let's have a look at a real-life example from my portfolio with some actual numbers:

I saw this house on the market for £69,950.

Using the method, we've discussed. I worked out the end value to be £85,000, and the rent at £500 plus a bit extra for the garage at the back.

The refurbishment appeared to be £5,000 (it later became £6,500 due to some bad builders).

Tej Talks

My buying costs were £2,241, consisting of Stamp Duty + Legal fees, no survey.

You might think what you can offer is: £85,000 minus buying costs, minus refurbishment = £77,759.

However, the remortgage would give me 75% of £85,000 which is £63,750. Ideally, we don't want to be putting too much more cash in the deal than this. Therefore, there is no way we could offer the original sum we calculated of £77,759. Because, once the property was purchased and refurbished, it would leave a large chunk of money, reducing your ROCLI and ability to recycle cash quickly.

When I say 'Cash into' the deal, it doesn't necessarily mean your personal money, it just means the total costs. Which in this case currently are the buying, holding, and refurbishing costs, this doesn't complete the picture though, we need to add purchase price.

To make this a deal which pulls out practically all the money put in. We want to reach £63,750 as our 'all-in' cost.

Therefore:

£63,750 (total remortgage) MINUS £2241 (buying costs), MINUS £5,000 (refurbishment cost), EQUALS = £56,509.

Is this what we can offer? What have we missed out?

Holding costs. Let's assume £25 a month insurance, and £0 Council Tax (you can be exempt whilst refurbishing a property), and let's just say you're paying 0.5% a month to an investor and it will take 6 months, so 3% of interest on the total money they've given you,

£63,750). Do not miss these out, they can become costly and they form a part of your deal.

At 6 months the holding costs are (6x£25 insurance, 6x£0 CT, and 6x£319 interest) = £2,064

So, £56,509 MINUS £2,064 EQUALS £54,445.

£54,445 is what your ideal offer would be, to leave almost £0 in the deal. However, I'm happy to leave £5,000 in so I can go up on this offer, but importantly I also have scope for my refurbishment to go up in cost, if needed. I'm looking for a 50% ROCLI.

Money left in is calculated as all the money you have spent, minus the remortgage amount. In this example, the remortgage amount of £85,000 is £63,750, and I have spent £63,750. Therefore, no money is left in this deal. Had I spent say £70,000, with the same remortgage, I would be leaving £6,250 in the deal. The diagram below visualises these splits.

I know this is a lot to take in, highlight stuff, come back to this, take a break, this is the foundation you need to go and find these deals.

If you go to tej-talks.com/sheet, then I will send you my spreadsheet and you can play with the figures above, or your own deals, and look at the formulae behind it to understand how it all links. A spreadsheet is your best friend for deal analysis, feel free to create your own too.

[CASE STUDY 3] – 227TYN

Want the full story of the deal above? Here goes, I spoke to the agent, offered £51,000, which was rejected. I then met the agent on another viewing a few weeks later, and she said that the vendor is looking for a quick sale, and she would consider a better offer. I upped my offer to £54,000, and it was accepted right away. It only came up via conversation that I created, I won't pretend and say we had a great relationship and she called me as soon as. I led this conversation.

Purchase Price: £54,000
Stamp Duty (SDLT): £1,620
Conveyancing Fee: £621
Refurbishment: £6,500
Interest on Finance: £4,514
Total money in: £67,832

RICS Valuation: £90,000

Remortgage Amount (75% LTV): £67,500

Money left in*: £332

Monthly
Rent: £525
Mortgage Cost: £205
Insurance Cost: £20
Cash flow/Profit: £300

Annual Cashflow/Profit: £3,340
ROCLI: 1,007%

Tej Talks

During writing this book, I actually had this remortgaged at £90,000, not £85,000, and it actually left in only £332! So, I've updated the case study, so it won't match the previous example exactly. My spreadsheet shoes holding costs, which are not detailed here to keep it simpler, so my figures look worse than yours may if you did quick maths.

By now, you have your goals set and the minimum Return On Investment you are happy with, this all combines to form a 'gold standard deal structure' that you can apply. Your new structure allows you to offer the right amounts on deals every time. I'd advise you to re-read or write out the deal structure we went through above, **it's vital you understand it.**

Let's talk about fundamentals. So far, I've covered what I look for in a deal on the money and numbers side, but I'm not buying any old house, in the middle of a field, off the grid somewhere. I look for other factors too, I've listed all the things I advise you to consider, I look at most, but not all of these.

Fundamental/Economical factors when buying BTLs:
- Located in a desirable area with low crime, clean streets and tidy houses
- Driving distance (or closer) to major supermarkets and amenities
- Parking for at least 1 car (unless City Centre)
- Areas of economic growth
- Regeneration projects occurring or planned
- Historic and/or expected capital appreciation
- Avoid local crime hotspots or bad-reputation areas
- Strong rental demand
- Strong sales demand
- Close to local schools

- Close to employers
- Areas considered 'nice to live' locally
- Gut feel when in the area, how does it feel?

Most of this can be researched using the wonderful world of Google, it's available for free online.

A few notes on other types of Property:

Council Estates - I avoid buying here, and even on ex-council estates, despite the houses here often being well built, I just find the tenant type doesn't match my overall strategy in my area. That's my view and experience, yours could be totally different.

New builds - I don't touch them, they don't make sense for my BRR model, they sound great and shiny and buying off plan seems great, if that's what you want to do then please do further reading into it, and make sure you understand the security of your money and deposit.

Flats - I don't buy these as they don't work out well in my areas, unless I convert a commercial or large residential to flats, which I'm looking at doing very soon. I also prefer Freehold to Leasehold; however, these can still work with the BRR model.

BUYING

find it - fund it

We have reached the first element of this model. So far; we have established our goals, what a deal looks like, and the figures we are aiming to achieve, with an understanding of the foundations that support this. I'm going to cover how to FIND it and FUND it. I'll show you what has been the most fruitful for me. You should test and analyse, be efficient and use the methods that provide you with a healthy pipeline, if one way doesn't work for you then cut it off.

FIND IT

The ways you can source property are:
- Online platforms
- Estate agents
- Lettings agents
- Auctions
- D2V Marketing
- Your network and social media
- Deal Sourcers

I advise you to use most, if not all of the above at the same time. It may seem like a lot but as you learn more, you'll see that a balanced and varied approach won't take all of your time and will produce results equal to your efforts. I'm going to cover a few of them in detail, and the rest I will discuss broadly as we could be here forever!

Some people claim that if a deal has reached an online platform, then it's too late, it's not a deal and unworthy of their time. This is totally incorrect, yes you want off-market deals direct to you, at a good price before the competition starts, but that doesn't mean deals are not right there in plain sight. You can and will find deals that work online, in the same places everyone is looking. It's not always how you found it, but how you secure it and take it through a process. People are put off by the listed price, that's not always the price a vendor will accept, the price is not set in stone and there's a few factors to consider here. Ideally all your deals will come straight to you, but please, don't be put off using websites to search for deals, as part of your toolkit.

Online Platforms
Let's start here, the easiest way to find properties and research areas, all from the comfort of your own home and mobile device. Most of the time, these properties will be listed with an Estate Agent, but I've separated this, as working with them needs a whole section.

I'll assume basic knowledge of using online property portals, if you need any help on this then I cover it in my eLearning, but they do make them easy to use.

I use Rightmove, Zoopla and On The Market, the biggest three in the UK to search for property, I use certain search parameters but once I've found a search I like, I will create an email alert ('Instant') so that the newest or reduced properties are sent straight to my inbox automatically, pretty handy. Rightmove is my favourite as the interface is so clear and you can save searches using drawn maps. Once you know your area well, you can make this search very specific, avoiding certain streets if you like, or have a search that follows a train line for example.

I keep my searches fairly open, I'm specific on areas but I won't select the bedroom filter, or type of house, I will put a maximum price in the search to stop it showing me all the big, nicely done houses, or those too expensive to fit my strategy. For example, in case study 4, I know the end values around there are £80,000 to £110,000 depending on the street, so my max price will be set at £90,000, because from experience I know I want to be buying way below that, to take into consideration refurbishment and other costs, in order to use the BRR model.

Anything above this won't be in bad enough condition. I set it quite high because many vendors will force the agent to list what they think it's worth, when we know it's worth a lot less. You may see a wreck of a house listed at £89,000, but you'll know it's not worth that and the price is not realistic, and if you set your 'max' price too low, then you'll miss these potential deals. This is something that you will refine over time.

Now most or all of the search results will not work for us, they will be too nice for us, i.e. we can't add any value with a refurbishment, and the listed price is accurate. Don't be disheartened, this is why we set alerts, because the same search in a few hours or days, can and will yield different results which could be more beneficial to you. If I click on a property and it looks interesting, or I'm going to call the agent, I will press the 'save' button, as it helps me keep track of what I've seen and if it gets sold then comes back on, you will remember it better.

Set alerts and use multiple platforms, they don't always overlap with listings and I find OnTheMarket often has listings that are not on the other two.

This is also an opportunity to practise and refine your deal analysis. Once you've read the whole book and we have been through refurbishments, you will be able to estimate rough build costs from the pictures, and you'll work out the end value, and know the costs. Therefore, before going on a viewing you can have a very rough idea of what your potential offer could be. This also helps you to understand if a property is worth viewing. If a (non-new) listing only has external pictures, then it's either tenanted or it's a total wreck and the agent isn't showing it to generate viewing interest. Always ask if they have photos, sometimes there's a totally unrelated reason.

I'll use an extreme example to explain this; A house listed at £100,000, requiring a huge refurbishment at £45,000, the end value is £110,000, and your spreadsheet says you have to offer £30,000 for it to work as a BRR. Yes, the vendor *may* accept an offer like this, but realistically, a £70,000 discount if the property is listed right, is unlikely. However, don't over-analyse and then never even go on a viewing. I've achieved pretty big discounts on property I honestly thought would never go for so cheap. Once you have read this book, this bit will become clearer. It may sound contradictory, and that's because it can be, it varies so much on every single house, so I want to give you a general and broad view.

If you're seeing something online, then so are many other people so you have to be quick in analysing, making contact/organising a viewing and offering. I've had houses come on at 4pm Tuesday, I called 10AM Wednesday and it was offer-accepted and listed as SOLD-STC. You want to be the person who that house is being sold to, speed is very important. When you get email alerts, review them straight away and make arrangements to view, this is a high priority task that can have tight time frames. However, some properties will sit on the market for months, and go nowhere, this indicates a disparity in the price the vendor wants, and what the market values the house at, there is still potential here. You would be surprised how many of these float about and don't get much interest, my first deal had been on the market for 6 months at £79,995 (the end value was £80,000 and it needed some work) but I secured it for £50,000.

Sounds silly right? It happens, and as you see from my case studies *(full pictures and videos on my website)* this is not uncommon. Persistence is very important in securing deals. That leads me nicely to my next section, most of these properties are going to be listed on platforms by

Estate Agents, so how do you convert an online listing into a set of keys for you?

Estate Agents

What does that make you think? Overconfident 18-year olds with pink striped shirts and a navy suit and tassels on their shoes, short sides and big quiff? That's the classic stereotypical image. But the majority I have met are knowledgeable, realistic and good fun to talk to. They haven't been cocky or arrogant like the perception may be, now this will vary in areas, but I do invest across a pretty big patch. It can seem daunting walking into an Estate Agent - it is at first, everyone clicking away, on the phones and you bumble in trying to be a 'serious investor!' This is why I don't just walk in for the first interaction, especially not with donuts or other high-sugar foods, like a lot of Property Courses would advise. I find that awkward.

Estate agents are the main place people go to sell their house, and it's the first place you look to buy a house, right?

They can be your sole source of deals because they are powerful allies to have, especially as you build strong relationships with them, trust me, you want to devote time to Agents. The information, local knowledge and properties I have acquired here is priceless. I've also had a lot of fun with them, don't forget the human side of all this bricks and mortar.

I like to make my first contact with an Agent on the viewing itself. So, I'll find a property online, then speak to the agent, preferably on the phone as voice is more memorable than a plain email. It also gives you an opportunity to chat and learn about other houses you could view.

Here is how the first conversation usually goes

Tej: "Hey, my name is Tej and I saw the property on XX Street, I wondered if it's still available to view?"

Agent: "It sure is, when would you like to see it?"

Tej: "Perfect, before I book it in, do you mind if I ask you a few questions about it?"

Agent: "Of course"

Tej: "How long has it been on the market? Why hasn't it sold yet? Has it had any offers?"

Agent: "About 2 months now, well houses can take time to sell and none of the offers have been what the vendor wants"

Tej: "Interesting, I know you can't tell me the exact offers, but what region are we talking about to have a shot here?"

Agent: (will either tell me exact numbers) or "Around the YY Region I think"

Tej: "Thank you, hmm, it looks like it needs a lot of work, does the vendor realise the scope of refurb? Is it as bad as the pictures?"

Agent: "yeah but they have a price they have to sell it at, so that's that, do you still want to view"?

Tej: "Sure, let's book it in for XX, out of interest if I refurbished this to a high standard, and gave it back to you to sell for me, what would you be confident selling it for?"

Agent: "Looking at recent data we estimate £YY - £YY"

Tej: "Thanks, I thought the same, actually whilst we are on the phone, what other properties do you have for sale in a similar condition? I like the ones that need some TLC. Have you seen anything with Subsidence? Cracks? Knotweed? Sticking on the market? Repossessions?"

Agent: "Now that you mention it, we have a few, let me send you an email with details and call me back if you want to view any of them, I'll also add you to the mailing list".

Tej Talks

Let's breakdown some of the key elements of this conversation:

- I'm asking if it's available to view, I'm not assuming it's still on the market as things go quick
- I want to know the story of the house, and what offers have been rejected, so I can see if what I'm thinking of is unrealistic so far or in line with those
- By asking why it hasn't sold yet, it can reveal information like "A previous seller had a survey and discovered XYZ"
- I ask if the vendor knows the work needed, because I can gauge if they are realistic or dreamers, and therefore how they may handle my offer
- I ask what they would sell it for, not what they think it's worth. I'm 1. Putting them in the firing line, so they may be more honest 2. I'm getting their local area knowledge and seeing if my data supports it and 3. I'm suggesting there's more commission in this conversation than just one sale, who doesn't like more money!
- I ask about other properties, but I don't stop there - I mention common 'red flags' on properties that will put most buyers off. I use certain words to trigger their memory to reveal what they may forget if I had asked one generic question. I've had deals from this technique alone.
- This whole conversation I am being myself, so if a listing is at a silly price, or the pictures are amusing, I'll bring it up because life is supposed to be fun! It also makes you more memorable out of 10s of other Investors.

Please note, this conversation varies every time and you have to adapt and ask questions pertinent to the information they are sharing and think on your feet. This isn't a script that works like magic, but it shows you what I'm doing at this early stage. It also helps you understand why I ask certain things, and in what way. On my eLearning, we go through these roleplays where you can hear my tone of voice. *How* you say something matters too, don't forget that. You also need to sound confident, warm and friendly on the phone, practise with a friend or in the mirror first. When they ask if you're a cash buyer, if you have access to your own funds, Investor money or Bridging Finance, then the answer is yes.

Once we have viewed a property and you have worked out the refurbishment (section on both later) it is time to make an offer. An offer that will very likely be rejected, just saying.

Here is how I would write a basic offer to an agent:

Hi [agent name],

Thanks for showing me around, great to chat to you today [include a personal detail from your convo here]!

I've calculated the numbers on this deal, and my offer is based on the following:

- Property is in a dire state and requires a lot of cost to bring up to standard
- £XXX for replastering and removing all the vendors rubbish
- £XXX for decorating and fitting the kitchen & bathroom
- £XXX for a rewire as the electrics are not safe
- £XXX for a new GCH system, as it doesn't have one
- The total spend required is £XXXX.

With an end value of £YYY, this leaves no profit for me as a business at asking price.

My offer is £XXX,XXX cash. 28 day completion.

My solicitor details are: Solictior@legalstuff.com, Proof of Funds and ID are attached.

Please let me know if we can proceed, my solicitor is ready.

******

As your relationship gets better, your offers will be less formal, and you won't need to add all the description above. It's important at the start, so they see you aren't offering stupid amounts with no rationalisation or evidence to support your price. I give my Solicitor details to show that I am ready to go and not messing around, anyone can have a Solicitor, but it just makes the offer feel more serious. I also attach Proof of Funds (PoF) even if they haven't asked, I'm showing money and the ability to take action here, it's important to assert that you have buying power.

Another tip is, even if I'm not offering on a property we viewed, I will email the agent with my PoF and ID, just to say please keep it on file for future offers. What I'm really doing is saying, go on, have a look at the funds in my account, I have money to spend and some of this will be your commission if you find me deals. I'm asserting my buying power very passively and getting them more intrigued by me without doing much. This works best when you have cash in an account, as opposed to an Agreement in Principle from a broker, which is more effective on a direct offer as it's usually dated and has the property address.

The most important part of finding deals online and through estate agents is the follow up.

A F U

Always Follow Up. I've spoken to so many people who do a few viewings here and there, put in offers, and then the agent never hears from them again. You need a system, a method of tracking all your offers, the date sent, what it was, what the feedback was and when you will contact them again about the offer.

You want the agent to remember you, and strongly associate you with that deal. If it gets sold, and then the seller pulls out (25% of Sales fell through in 2019), you want the agent to think of you right away and call you or you want to have followed up recently. The majority of my Agent deals have come through following up, I've only had 1 offer accepted first time, which speaks volumes. You could set up a Virtual Assistant to follow up from a spreadsheet tracker, that's what I've done.

In general, estate agents' value (in no particular order) these in an investor:
- Honesty
- Commitment
- Punctual
- Interesting to talk to
- Proof of funds
- Potential to buy multiple properties
- Polite and friendly interactions
- Not wasting their time
- 'Sensible' or evidenced offers

It's not rocket science. Don't come off a property course and walk into an agency with a box of shit donuts, claim you're a hot shot investor and you want to be on their exclusive Investor list right away. This is a relationship, so treat it accordingly because it can be very fruitful for both of you. At the same, don't treat them like they are gods and know it all, often you will have a lot more knowledge than them about property investing, don't be cocky with it but don't be intimidated by them. Remember, money talks - you'll notice the more houses you buy; the smoother things will go with them and the more deals you have access to. Be patient, and consistent.

I will give gifts to an agent if they have been helpful, and we've completed a purchase. Usually a nice card saying thanks and some confectionery. I prefer to be thoughtful about it, i.e. if they like Protein bars then I'll get them that.

Over time, your relationship will be at a point where they come to you with deals before they go online, or they give you a heads up on their pipeline. This happens when you put your money where your mouth is - when you buy houses from them. Once you have proved you are an active buyer, who completes quickly on all offers accepted, they will want to work with you more. If they have visibility of your brand, that can also be powerful because they will see your growth in real-time, and maybe even want a slice of the action. I could do with a slice of Pizza right now.

Letting Agents
This is a very small section, because by their nature they are not selling property, however they are managing for landlords. Some of these will want to retire or have bad tenants and want to get rid of the house, the first people to know about this is their agent. Build relationships with them, whether it's as direct as saying you will buy properties off tired

landlords happily. Or, if they manage your property, slip it into conversations and check in regularly. If they or their Sales Department could make a cut of a direct sale, with no marketing, viewings etc involved, it makes their life a lot easier. Great situation for all.

Don't expect to find houses in terrible condition here, therefore, most are unlikely to work for BRR. You may even come across portfolios for sale at a discount. If you do find something in a terrible state, I'd have some opinions about the letting agent… this is a topic for another day!

Some lettings agents are independent and very well networked, one of mine will regularly send me property from his landlords, or Sourcers, or people he knows locally. All he wants in return is the management of the property, which is fair and beneficial.

Auctions
Caveat Emptor.

"Let the buyer beware"

This is a really important phrase. In auctions the risk of a deal not stacking, or the house suffering serious problems can be increased compared to Agent purchases. I'm starting with this, because I want you to understand the extra risk that Auctions bring. This is not to put you off, but to have this at the front of your mind as you read on. They are a great place to get deals, and I think they should be a part of your strategy. But I want you to see it from all sides. Go and visit one, just sit there and observe.

Auctions exist for a few reasons:
- Allow vendors a quick and secure sale
- Repossession disposal

Tej Talks

- Selling structurally damaged property
- Selling property with legal difficulties
- Selling non-standard or other unmortgageable property
- Transparency of the transaction for certain seller-types
- Vendors can entice people in with a low guide price
- No chain issues

On the day of auction, as soon as the gavel falls, you have legally exchanged. You need 10% minimum, usually on a debit card to pay the deposit. The timer now starts, normally 28 days (can be anything) to completion. Come prepared, if you're bridging or using investor finance, get it pre-approved or agreed. You are locked in to purchase. Sure, you can pull out and sacrifice the deposit, but the seller can sue you for costs and the price difference if they then have to sell it at a lower price. Ouch.

Viewings are usually done in blocks and as open houses, meaning anyone is welcome to attend. Check with the auction house, as you may have to book beforehand so they can track numbers. I find these fun, good places to check out the competition and network. I've met interesting people here. You also learn a lot just by listening to general conversations in the properties, there's local knowledge you may not know about. Just be weary that people are not talking aloud to feed false information to put you off. Be extra cautious on these viewings, as there will be properties that are complete wrecks, so you need to analyse the potential refurbishment cost properly, and account for the unknown. Also, I've been to places with gaping holes in the floor, snapping floorboards and fire damage, where you could seriously injure yourself.

Proceed with caution.

Take hand sanitiser too, lord knows you'll need it, some of these houses be stanky...

Once the viewing is done, it's up to you to do your DD on the deal as usual, don't forget to add in any auction fees that they add (check small print). People ask me if they should get a surveyor in to assess an auction property. I personally don't find surveyors useful for the houses I buy. I've found my own knowledge built over time, combined with a very experienced Builder and the internet, to be more than sufficient to diagnose issues. I am fascinated by construction though, so I have taken the time to learn things. Surveyors will mention everything bad with the house and overestimate costs, to protect their insurance liability. It can be costly, especially at auction where the chances of you winning a specific Lot are not high, you could be spending £1000s. You could argue the cost of a bad deal is more than that, and I'd agree somewhat. This doesn't apply to everyone, if there are serious structural issues and you are confident you can secure it, then get an engineer or surveyor in, but don't let that 'sunken cost' on their fees lead you to overpay at auction. Also, I must state that best practise is to get a Surveyor in, for the protection of your business and funds.

The legal pack is a collection of documents that would normally be created by the seller's solicitors during the conveyancing process, and the buyer's solicitors who prepare the Searches. I love this element of auctions, legally everything is *(or should be)* upfront early on. This means another level of DD, allowing you to decide early on if this property is right for you. This should mean, you don't need to pull out because somethings been discovered later down the line. However, that does happen sometimes. It can also give you an insight as to why the property is for sale, any physical and/or legal issues it may have. Personally, I find Legal Packs straightforward to read on freehold BTLs and out of the 5 I've got from auction, none of them have had any issues legally. However, as best practise I don't recommend this unless you are legally trained. If you contact me, I can introduce you to my solicitors who will read it for you, at a fair rate, and if you are successful you then get a reduced conveyancing fee. Also, you'll soon come to dislike the sellers Solicitor, as they will have a requirement in the Special Conditions that you pay their fee, which will miraculously double or even triple compared to the norm, even though the work is less than normal. Why? Because they can, it's normal and they are annoying. Again, I must state that best practise is to get a solicitor to read legal packs. Nothing that I have written or said constitutes legal advice. Please see independent legal advice.

Right, you've done your DD, the legal pack is satisfactory, and you are ready to bid. You must set a maximum bid before you enter that room, and you must not diverge from it. There's two ways I set my bids:

- *One maximum bid*
Let's say on my spreadsheet I can't afford to pay more than £150,000. This is the number I bid up to, and I will not go any higher. When you first go to auctions, I suggest sticking to this, as auctions become more natural and you are in control, I personally would go up slightly on my max bid, because I know my emotions are in check and it's a 28 day easy completion. I will pay a little extra for the speed and certainty. However, if your ego will carry you away or you're afraid of overpaying, then stick to this bid, don't play with fire when you haven't got water.

- *Three bids, with play between them*
Best bid, middle bid, and worst-case bid. £140,000 is best case, £150,000 is middle and worse case is £160,000 for example. Each of these figures works on your spreadsheet, but by having 3 checkpoints

on the way up, it can give you time to assess the situation and step back early if needed. This can also make the emotional impact less, as it breaks bidding into easier stages.

When you're in the room, stand at the back or sides. You want to see the entire room, who's bidding so you can stick your tongue out at them... just kidding, well sort of. Psychological factors come into it here, the way you bid, speak, gesture, even the figures you bid to can all encourage or put some off from bidding. The transparency and free for all structure is really fun, and I've certainly put others off from my bidding style before. At the end, stay and network, try and speak to the Auctioneer, shake their hand and start building rapport, introduce yourself.

How many others are doing this? It's not difficult to stand out when others aren't even trying!

Online bidding is different, I think it's easier to overspend here because it's all digital and it doesn't feel real, it's numbers on a screen going up, like buying with a credit card over cash.

"Before the hammer falls" By Jay Howard & Piotr Rusinek - this book has helped me, and I owe some of the above knowledge to them and I've made £1000s from the advice in their book. Buy it!

D2V Marketing

This simply means Direct to Vendor, so instead of going through a portal, website, agent or 'middle-person' you are engaging the owner (vendor) directly and negotiating with them. These deals are often 'Off-Market', you'll hear this online and it seems to be the Holy Grail of deals, because no one else has seen it or has access to it. It is great as it could be exclusively with you, meaning no competition, direct negotiation and the seller doesn't have agency fees or interference (not always a good thing).

I find agents great and working with them can be easier as it's more transactional and less emotional like it can be with vendors. It's also in an agent's best (financial) interests to secure offers and push conveyancing along, so it's nice to have a third party speeding it up. With vendors you may spend a lot of time, having a lot of meetings with emotional discussions, that end up nowhere. You can't rush these, as it could be someone's prized possession, an investment gone wrong, a deceased family member's house and/or somewhere that has a lot of memories and value to them. Despite the condition perhaps not matching their perceived value, which is where your negotiation comes in.

Common methods of D2V Marketing:
- Leafleting via letterboxes
- Direct Letters
- Newspaper/Magazine adverts
- Radio adverts
- Google AdWords adverts
- Facebook paid adverts
- 'Bandit Boards'
- Posters in the windows of your projects in Refurbishment
- Posters on community boards or in newsagents
- Speaking to Neighbours giving them your business card
- Asking around in local builders merchants
- Telling your builders to keep an eye out
- Family and friends
- Council disposals

There are many ways to contact vendors, I wouldn't recommend doing them all as it will be very time consuming and expensive and may not yield an efficient result. I suggest picking 1-3 (some overlap) and using them alongside the other methods outlined here.

Quick tips: Leafleting - you can do this yourself, but it's incredibly boring and time consuming, these hours could be spent finding deals or Investors. To send direct letters using the vendors name, you can pay £3 per address on the Land Registry to find their details. Asking the neighbours is very powerful, knock and introduce yourself, explain you are refurbishing next door and apologise for any noise/disturbance. Give them your number and say they can call you with any issues, then ask if they know anyone looking to sell? (and looking to rent/buy, for your house).

As usual, expect big numbers going out (like with viewings) and small numbers coming in, this isn't a magical method of sourcing, but it certainly does work. When discussing with the Vendor, it's two ears one mouth - listen and ask, what do they need, what do they want, what's their situation and how can you help? Sometimes you won't be able to do anything apart from give some advice or refer them to someone in your network. The ideal is to meet them face to face, to strengthen the relationship, make you more memorable and to help you stand out. However, if you invest far from home, this may not be practical so consider a pre-screening questionnaire to go through on the phone. Make use of technology and ask for pictures to be sent via Whatsapp, you may get people with new houses wanting to sell, and this doesn't fit our strategy, images will make that clear very quickly.

It's best to go to the meetings equipped with as much information as possible about the end value, rentability and saleability in the area, you can then make better decisions in this meeting. Remember, both parties should have a positive outcome from any deal agreed.

Email your local council housing department and ask if they have a mailing list for any of their disposals, or how you can have access to them. There are some amazing deals here, but you have to be quick.

Your network
You never know who has money, deals, or a bit of both in today's world. Never judge a book by its cover - they say - and I've often found it to be solid advice.

Most of your network will likely be Property Investors like you, so, why would they have any deals to pass on? It doesn't hurt to ask the question, and tell everyone what you're looking for, always. I've had deals sent to me for free, from agents, friends, Investors - anyone, and I always think of someone I like who I know is looking for that, to make a referral. Here's some examples of what I've received, so you see what's possible:

- Friend secured a house D2V but couldn't purchase it. Was agreed at £35,000, with a £15,000 refurbishment and an £80,000 end value. That's a great BRR, no money left in. He called me and said I don't want a fee, but I'll pass you the deal. Unfortunately, the vendor became irrational and silly and it wasn't worth working with him.

- Letting agent sends me 2 houses to buy together, off-market from one of his Landlords. Market value £163,000, asking £133,000.

- Builders speaking to locals in the community and sending me 4 potential deals, off-market and D2V.

- An Estate Agent recognised me from Instagram, talking about me in their Branch meeting, and sending me exclusive information about deals pre-market, and represents me better to his Vendors as the trust is built from my Brand. Secured my SA unit from him.

Just a few examples, but anyone you meet, and I mean anyone, anywhere could bring you deals or be an Investor. So, tell everyone what you do, and what you're looking for. Offer to pay introduction fees too - if you complete on a Property, they found you.

Deal Sourcers

Sourcers are people who bring you secured deals and look after the refurbishment for you and some even take it to market for sale or letting. They allow you to invest in places far from home with much less of a time commitment than doing it yourself. They should be providing better deals than you'd find yourself, taking your time and effort into consideration. They can be a very powerful part of your team.

This is last on the list for a reason, this shouldn't be your first method of finding deals if you are full-time property, even if you're part time you may not need them. However, some of you reading this will be cash rich, time poor and want to own assets as opposed to passively investing like my investors do. Therefore, you may need someone to vet, buy, and refurbish the houses for you, what's called a 'turnkey' investment and Sourcers can provide this. For example, if you work 9-5 in the city, you go home and its family time, rinse and repeat every day every week, you may have no free time. Consider a sourcer in situations like this.

Tej Talks

I find most Sourcers to be overpriced, lazy, and lacking diligence. Go on Rightmove, see a deal at £100,000 asking, let's offer £97,000 and slap on a £3,000 sourcing fee… technically it's still below market value, but see what they did there? Sorry to any good sourcers reading this, you bad sourcers feel free to @ me on socials, I'm ready. A lot of Sourcers see sourcing as a steppingstone to building relationships and then buying houses themselves and/or quitting their jobs. That's great, seriously it's the best way to get started, but when it's treated like this and lacks the attention it deserves, it causes issues. It's too easy to do the above, or secure things just below asking and then sell to someone out of the area, who either doesn't mind that or doesn't understand the figures themselves. If you get sent a deal by a Sourcer, go online and see if it is there, and what the asking price is and if it's really been secured.

Sourcing has a low barrier to entry; it doesn't take much to set up. What this means is, you'll get a higher proportion of bad apples in every batch of good ones. Keep your wits about you, and don't be afraid to question everything or turn down deals.

This is a vital relationship if you need it, especially if the Sourcer is any good at Project Management (PM is not an easy role to just pick up). Keep them on side and work closely with them, they could build you an empire, at a cost yes, but if you don't have the time or inclination to do it, then it's all good and part of the bigger picture.

Here's what I think makes a good Sourcer:
- Understand the local area and market
- Honest about figures, realistic expectations and understands Property
- Good relationships with Estate/Letting Agents
- Refurbishment costs are broken down line by line

Tej Talks

- They take their sourcing fee into consideration when calculating ROI %
- Clear pictures and video tour of the Property with commentary
- Present solid comparable properties to evidence their end value
- Genuine discount
- Preferably using some off-market or D2V sourcing methods, not just portals
- Has secured the deal SOLD STC, not still listed on the market
- Has Project Managed successful refurbishments before
- Taken a project from sourced, to refurbishment completion for multiple customers

Don't pay a sourcer for an auction property, what's the point? Makes no sense to me. Pay someone else to view it for you, and then the rest is your diligence and an open bidding on the day, which can be done online or on the phone.

Sourcers need to be compliant:
- Registered with Property Ombudsman or Property Redress Scheme
- Applied for or registered with HMRC for Anti-Money Laundering (AML)
- GDPR Compliant and ICO members
- Professional Indemnity Insurance (minimum £100,000 cover)

You can find sourcers at networking events and on social media, I would suggest using one with an established or strong personal brand, it gives some 'public liability' if things go wrong and they don't handle it properly. Talk to a range and analyse their deals and attitudes, don't rush in and make a decision too early. I've done Podcasts with a few sourcers before, have a listen and see what you think.

Now you've found a deal, how are you supposed to pay for it? I will talk you through the methods of funding your deals. I could write a whole book on working with private investors and JVs, so I have made these sections very efficient and lean, giving you only the most important elements.

FUND IT
- Cash
- Bridging loan
- Mortgage
- Private investor loan
- Joint Venture
- Pension funds (SSAS)

Cash
Does what it says on the tin, if a house costs £100,000 and you have this in your bank account, and you use it all to purchase the house, it would be a cash purchase. This means the house is unencumbered, so it has no mortgages on the house and usually no charges or restrictions. This is considered a safer way to buy, as there is no debt. It also means a lump of cash is tied up, until you refinance or forever if you just leave it as is. No fees as it's your own money and potentially cheaper legal fees.

Bridging
You could split that £100,000 into four £25,000 deposits, and buy four houses for £100,000 each, using bridging finance to make up the rest (£75,000 at 75% LTV). So, it's great for multiplying the current cash you have, and making it work harder. More fees, more process, but can

still be quick. They will take a charge on the property, so it's less secure for you. It's a very powerful method of buying. You can even bridge on an unencumbered property that you purchased with cash to 'capital raise' and pull money out of it. It will be more expensive than a mortgage, and maybe more-so than a private investor, with some companies there are lots of hidden fees. Please, be careful and read every line of the terms.

Bridgers will usually take a first charge, personal guarantee, company debenture and ensure you take 'Independent Legal Advice'. They aren't stupid, they will use every form of security above and beyond just the basics to secure their funds. Speak to your Solicitor about the risks here. You can also do 'Open Market Value' or End-Value bridges, where they loan based on the finished value, after your refurbishment. So, you may get more than the usual 75% LTV, speak to your Bridger or broker about it. Please be careful when using Bridging and understand the risks.

Mortgages

In the BRR strategy you should not be buying at the start with a mortgage, so many people ask me this, as they want to save money on the fees and interest. How tight is the deal or how unrealistic are your expectations that it can't handle fees? Sure, you could do this and maybe get away with it, a few times, but mortgages are long-term products, so they aren't supposed to be redeemed so quickly. I do not advise this, use other methods. Some people like to buy with a residential mortgage on a small deposit, then switch it over. You can't do this with a Ltd company and you then lose your first-time buyer stamp duty relief, which you may want to save for your own home, which will probably cost more than your investments. Also, it's just not the proper way to do it. I cover re-mortgaging in detail in the refinance section of this book.

Private Investor Loans

This is the primary way I have been able to grow so quickly, by working with people just like you, from a real variety of professional backgrounds. They loan me money, just like a bank or bridger would, I pay them an interest rate and return their money at the end of the term (usually 12 months). Some will loan 100% LTV and want a first charge; some will loan smaller amounts which you can use for a deposit when buying with a bridging loan. Or you could use smaller amounts for refurbishments, but just check the FCA rules on 'Collective Investment Schemes' and make sure you're compliant. I've met all of my Investors from social media, yes, that's right - my bright yellow t-shirt, posts and podcasts is what generated me £600,000 in just 5 months of raising finance. It took me 6+ months of building a brand to get to that point, but I'm not complaining. Borrow responsibly, speak to your solicitor about drawing up a loan agreement and running checks on your Investor, and read the FCA guidelines.

Joint Venture

This is where you and the investor, or anyone, holds equity or shares in a business that owns (to sell or hold) property. So, you are both liable when it goes wrong, and both responsible when it goes right. A lot of people will approach you, without knowing you and ask for a JV, it's silly. It's like a marriage, I think most of us would consider a relationship like that seriously, not just with randoms from the internet. This is a good way when you're starting out, as people may be more willing to JV than loan your money. I don't JV, I like clean cut, clear profit investor loans. JVs can be very profitable and go very well, they can also go up in flames and humans are a pain at the best of times, and when money is involved - it can get worse. You need an agreement here written by a Solicitor, protect yourself and your JV partners, I'll say it again, money reveals people's true characters, so be careful. Most people do a 50/50 split, but I see it differently. I see three key elements; 1. Time 2. Money 3. Deal/experience/build team. If I have number 1 and 3, and you bring 2, then you get a 33% share. Makes logical sense to me - what do you think?

SSAS

I haven't used these yet, but if you've been working in a job for a while and have built up a substantial pension pot, or your network has the same, this is a great method. Take control of your pension and utilise it effectively on property projects. There are good books on this topic and information online, check it out - you could be sitting on gold. Seek professional advice.

REFURBISH

put some sauce on it

REFURBISHMENT

Some would argue that this is the most challenging aspect of property. For me, I find it is an opportunity to showcase my creativity and have fun. This is the aspect you may be dreading: finding and working with builders, it can be a total nightmare and even at the best of times it is not easy, especially when investing from far. By the time you reach this stage your local network should be strong, which is going to prove vital in this stage, so do not neglect it, as they will be very useful in checking in on progress and snagging on your behalf. When you get the keys, sort out utilities, most houses I buy have historical debt on them and won't provide gas or electricity until cleared. Call the company, wait for hours with the dodgy hold-music, and they will clear it for free.

Assessing a property on your viewings

You need to create a viewing checklist for properties, I'd encourage you to do this digitally as it's much easier to track and also saves paper. When viewing a property, I spend most of the time talking to the agent, to build a relationship. When you are starting out, I suggest you focus more on the property itself as you may miss some issues, or not understand and this can be very costly. Over time the emphasis will shift, as you become more competent in assessing properties, and the relationship takes time-priority. I'm not saying you become careless, but you'll naturally walk into a lot of properties and be able to assess them quickly, due to experience.

You can set up a Google form that inputs data directly into a spreadsheet (could also be your viewings tracker) or via your CRM system. It's easy to do, and on a viewing, you easily input data whilst walking around, and taking pictures. Alternatively, a note-app like Evernote allows you to combine text, pictures and videos in the same document, making it convenient to refer back to you, especially if you forgot what a particular house looked like or you want to show your builder. I don't take my builder on viewings, because I'm usually accurate in my estimate, and they can give a rough idea from pictures/videos if needed. Most will not want to come along, as most of these viewings won't actually come to fruition.

Here's key things you need to be noting:

- Inspect the Gas/Central Heating/Hot Water system
- Inspect the electrical system and Consumer Unit
- Check all windows & doors – uPVC/Timber/etc.
- Assess for structural issues, bowing walls, cracks, subsidence
- Assess for damp – rising, water ingress etc.
- Inspect guttering, roof and chimney where possible
- Overall condition (paint, flooring, clean, issues)
- Wallpaper or plastered walls
- Floors bouncy or solid
- Woodwork condition & useability
- Kitchen & bathroom condition
- Condition of garden & presence of Japanese Knotweed

Want a free digital and easy-to-edit viewing checklist?

Leave a review for the book on Amazon, and for my Podcast on an Apple device or on the Facebook page, email me the proof and I will send it to you in an editable format. hey@tej-talks.com

[CASE STUDY 4] – 22VIC

Purchased at Auction and couldn't view it myself, so a property investor friend of mine did. It was a repossession with a 2-week completion, so I bridged this one with Investors money as I couldn't afford to wait. It's on the best street in a not so great area and is a big 4 bed which is unusual here. I missed big items off the refurbishment, as did my prior terrible Project Manager when he priced the job. But, I'm liable at the end of the day and that's the accountability we have to have as Investors.

Purchase Price: £45,000
Stamp Duty (SDLT): £1,350
Auction Fee: £600
Conveyancing Fee: £1,000
Refurbishment: £19,350
Interest on Finance: £3,645

Total money in: £71,474

Estimated value/sold price: £80,000

Remortgage Amount (75% LTV): £60,000

Money left in*: £11,474

<u>Monthly</u>
Rent: £600
Mortgage Cost: £175
Insurance Cost: £22
Cash flow/Profit: £343

Annual Cashflow/Profit: £3,880 **

116

ROCLI: 34%

I flipped this property instead of holding, as it doesn't meet my ROCLI standard and it leaves in too much money. I have an Investor to pay back! I also had one of my other proposed flips get a really high valuation in a great area, so I kept that instead. This will make a profit of c£6,000 after Agent & Legal fees so it's not making a loss, despite the issues. You have to adapt in Property, even if that means selling off an asset you hadn't planned to. The reason this refurbishment increased so much is the entire roof had to be redone, as the people before essentially covered it in Bitumen so it became one big sheet, and it was leaking. The rear render had to be done also, with the cost of scaffolding. I took too long to decide my course of action on this house.

I kept waiting, getting a few prices here and there. I was stuck, it was so clear looking back what I should have done – but I couldn't bring myself to spend the money and just get on with it. Had I done so, I'd have made more profit and had less headache. Reducing the time from problem to solution is so important. Often, we just have to spend the money and get over it.

Although the ROCLI is 34%, so it's not far off, it doesn't fit my business. I tried to sell with the roof and render not done, as an 'investor' property to do up, but as it was in a strange state with the inside finished and the outside not, it didn't sell or get enough interest in the trial listing. I hope this shows you things can go wrong no matter how diligent you are, but if you purchase at the right price, you may be able to save the deal. If you're following me on Instagram, you'll get the most up to date information on how some of these case studies have progressed @tej.talks

Tej Talks

Pricing up a Refurbishment

This is an area that I always get asked about, it's something that comes so naturally to me now because I love this part of property, but also because I'm a very curious person. If I don't know something, I will ask, if I don't understand the answer, I will ask again. If you can have the same curiosity and desire for knowledge, then you will pick up a lot of information that most people won't. I'm always learning, I'm by no means an expert - I still ask my builder questions and do my own research when needed.

I'm not giving you a standard list of prices for every detail in a refurbishment. This will vary in every area, between builders and on your specification, materials and end value of a house. For example if you just plasterboard a house it will cost X, but what if you have to use fire board, elements board and impact boards in certain places, plus some damp proofing behind the boards, it's going to cost you a lot more than X. The same goes for fitting a low-end kitchen with a laminate worktop, to a custom built one with a Quartz worktop, yes, the latter is unlikely to be in a rental, but you could be doing that in your Flips. I also think this is an important part of your property journey, to experience different quotes and understand how and why prices differ. I've seen some stark differences that made me laugh, I'm sure you'll see these too. Sometimes there is no rational explanation!

How to estimate refurbishment costs
- Speak to or get on the mailing list of local deal sourcers - a good deal pack will have a breakdown of the building works costs
- Call builders and ask them roughly what they charge for X, Y, Z (most will not do this without seeing the house, some may go off pictures)

- Use Social Media - ask 5 people locally how much it costs them to do certain jobs, and take the average as the figure you use in calculations
- There are only a few active Builders on Facebook, but find them and take them to lunch and pick their brains
- Once you have a property, get a few Builders around to quote, and ask for a breakdown of price
- A local Mentor can advise on build costs, if they are good
- Join an Earn & Learn programme with an active Property Investor
- Jewsons Aviator or Travis Perkins Estimator tools

These are great ways to get guideline figures for you to assess deals and price up refurbishments after viewings, to be able to offer on houses. Once you have purchased and you work with a build team, you can refine these, and get a complete price list off them.

Ideally, you want to be writing out a Schedule of Works, which is a document that explains each job to be done, to what level and the cost. A line by line breakdown of costs and each item in a Refurbishment. The level of detail is up to you, the more the better but don't overdo it. The builder usually fills in the cost, but if you can hand three builders the same SoW it means that when they provide you a quote, it's much easier to compare. It also means you can understand the real cost of each aspect, instead of one lump sum figure for the whole job that means absolutely nothing.

Finding good builders
You can find good builders using the following methods:
- CheckATrade, MyBuilder or Trust a Trader (online)
- Local trade counters at Builders Yards and Kitchen/Bathroom suppliers

- Google searches for their websites
- Facebook Business pages
- Networking events
- Social Media (i.e. Instagram)
- Walking into active sites you see in your area and saying hi
- Recommendations/Referrals

I value recommendations above all else, but don't accept it from anyone. Is the person making an introduction an Investor too? Have they worked with them before? What were the pros/cons? Why are they referring them to you instead of working with them more? You want a balanced view from the person, you won't ever have a 100% perfect review of a tradesperson, or any business, so be weary and ask lots of questions first.

Some people are highly unlikely to share their core builder with you, why would they? If they're keeping them busy, they would much rather keep them to themselves, so they don't get distracted or busy with other sites, slowing them down. I wouldn't share mine, given the volume I buy at - I can't afford to. However, many people are not buying at the same speed, or don't have enough work for their builder so they will share, it's always worth asking.

You'll find most builders use FB business pages instead of a website, and many are unlikely to be at networking events, but don't discount any of the methods. Your builder will make or break your refurbishment so take time and speak to a broad range of people. The trade counters can be quite a useful place, but again verify the person they recommend, is it just a business card left there, or have they used and seen their work multiple times.

Here are the kind of questions I like to ask builders when first vetting them:

- How long have you been in the business?
- How many refurbs do you reckon you have done?
- What's your preferred area of building, are you multi-skilled?
- How many trades do you have working under you and do they cover specific things?
- If things get really busy, how many more people can you recruit?
- Have you ever been kicked off or left a project?
- Tell me about a time you fell out with a client?
- What do you really hate with a client?
- How can I make your life easier as a builder?
- Do you prefer to earn slightly less on each job, but to have multiple and never have to pitch for the business?
- What insurance do you have? (Public Liability as a minimum)
- Will you work under a contract with me?
- I work to stage payments based on actual work completed - can you agree to this?

If they are annoying you already at this stage, or not being responsive then leave it here. Yes, Builders do get people who waste their time, as does anyone in business, but how they behave here is important. You also want to tell them about you, your experience and your plans, I told my team from day 1 I am going to buy 3 a month, so the work I have for you is potentially endless, if we work well, then I have no issues giving you it all. Only if we work well. I also offered to help with their branding and business if they wanted.

After your first chat, I advise visiting some active sites they are working on, and also looking at finished jobs, and speaking to previous clients. You're looking at the quality of work, how clean the site is and if things look botched or patched up, and how they describe things. If they say the owner wanted a quick fix, then you can't judge them off it but if they say it's a full fix and you can see it clearly isn't, that's a problem. Speaking to a client before can give you some insight into their working habits, if they finish jobs neatly and their communication skills. They could give you a fake number, so perhaps visit the person if possible.

I like to look at these things when judging builders:
- Neatness of tiling, grout lines, trims, levels and alignment
- Kitchen cabinets open/close smoothly, all level with no gaps and built sturdy
- Toilet works, taps work normally and there are no leaks
- Unsightly pipes hidden or painted over
- RCD box fitted neatly
- Plastered walls are smooth with no trowel marks
- Painted walls have even coverage with no patches, woodwork is smooth and the cutting in is straight and accurate
- Boilers fitted neatly with tidy pipes
- Doors open and close normally and fitted with 3 screws, and handles work smoothly
- Carpets/flooring fitted tight at the ends and no play underfoot
- No stupidity like an open electrical socket next to the shower or a cooker underneath a flammable surface etc (lack of common sense)
- Is the garden tidy or clean?
- Clean site

Just remember, the owner may request certain things that can make the builder look bad, so always clarify why something has been done and whose decision it was. Although, take answers with a skip of salt. No, not a pinch, that's what Harvester use to season their chicken.

Tej Talks

Ideally you will have a few people you are feeling good about, now is the time to send them a Specification or Schedule of Works, for a current build or future one, and ask them for a line by line price breakdown. Some will refuse as they often get time wasters, and some will complete it. Now you can compare the prices, why they differ and if the price change means a quality change.

Appointing a builder
Great! You've found a builder you'd like to work with, and they've passed all the checks we've been through. Do a little dance, celebrate, because it's bloody hard work... but it only gets harder. In this section I'm going to cover the basics you should set out from day 1, to ensure the rest runs smoothly.

Essentials are:
- Schedule of Works detailing every aspect to be completed and the prices
- Payment Schedule (this may vary with on-site issues/delays)
- Works agreed in a contract or very clear emails
- Agreement of who is sourcing the Swag like Kitchen/Bathroom
- No further work to be carried out without your written permission
- Agreement that 10% or more is being held until the house is snagged
- Their proof of PI Insurance and/or others

Have all the above in writing, whether it's a signed contract or an email stating the same, with them responding that they agree.

Make it clear you will not be paying any invoices without receipts or proof of work done to the right standard (pictures, videos or site visits).

If you're a distance investor, always say that someone will physically be checking the work. Don't say just send me pictures, don't create an environment where they can hide things and lie. Trust me, I've been lied to and numerous things totally hidden from me.

Managing builders

The real fun starts here (said no one ever). When working with a new builder trust needs to be built on both sides, and you will likely be anxious about them being any good. This is normal, use that anxiety to make you weary, question things and be on alert for issues. This is like any relationship; you learn what the other is like and adapt your communication when required. For example, I know a previous builder hates when any other trade comments on his work, so I always make a joke if I provide any feedback and/or I ask very openly with no hint of accusation. It's easy to be told XYZ by your carpet fitter and go straight to your builder and ask leading questions or sound angry, keep it neutral and be a mediator, not a fire starter. I also know some prefer texting, and the odd phone call if there is a serious issue or a broad topic to discuss.

You need to strike a balance between keeping a close eye, and regular updates without micromanaging, as that will irritate everyone. Discuss this with the builder, ask what they prefer, share what you'd like and ensure they agree with you. Be regimental with updates, every X day no matter what or every X item completed. I do stay in communication with my builder daily (I manage my refurbishments) and they know the importance of pictures for my brand to raise investment. This doesn't mean working with them is easy though. I've been burnt before, so I see trades as guilty before innocent, sorry but that's how I roll. It's a balance of feeling that, but not really showing them that.

My top tips for managing a builder:

- Agree a payment schedule from day one
- I don't pay anything upfront, materials or whatever I won't do, I offer to pay them daily for the first week if they need cash flow, but I expect them to have some funds for minor materials and I won't pay any labour upfront, never, ever. I will pay an hour after I've seen proof though, so I'm not harsh
- Understand and clarify their communication techniques
- Show that you trust them, but be careful and don't lose control
- Discuss serious issues F2F or on the phone, texts can be misconstrued
- Ask their opinion on parts of a refurb, they may not have one, but I've learnt so much this way
- If they suggest a fix or aspect of a refurb always ask if there is an alternative that is more effective
- Certain trades need to be registered ('Gas Safe Register' for Gas Engineers and a few bodies for Electricians) so check this before they do their bit (I've had a fake electric certificate before and a 'fake' rewire)
- Drop some snacks off when you visit site
- Do not give one team too much work, they will always claim they can handle it, this will be the downfall of their work with you. Trust me
- Hire slowly, fire fast

Materials

As you know, I love interior design and it's the most enjoyable part of Property for me. With single lets, there's not a huge amount of swag you can add compared to an HMO or SA. So, the focal points are the kitchen and bathroom. Doors, sockets/switches, carpets and wall colours come next in order of impact. All should be considered and be harmonious, comfortable and attractive. I'm not going to go through design in this book, as it is personal to you but there are many guides online, Pinterest and Instagram provide great ideas too. Just don't go overboard, it has to be durable too.

I don't let my Builders order or pick the Kitchen and Bathroom; I plan these carefully and use a variety of styles throughout my houses. Everyone does cheap gloss white with boring chrome handles, I'm sorry y'all but that is a little dull. Yes, it will still rent or sell, the demand is so high, but for the same price you can create a stylish space for your tenants, stand out to investors and push your rental price. I've done it before, multiple times. Yes, there is a limit to how far you should go on BTLs, area dependent but please, please, consider something other than white gloss slabs! There is nothing wrong with white, so maybe consider the finish, worktop, sinks, taps and handles that can make a normal kitchen look special. At the same time, I understand the need for these expensive items to be long lasting, and still look decent in 10 years. It's all a balance and I'm clearly fussy.

I source these myself and go directly for the suppliers, and I'm always on the lookout for new ones who can match price and service. I have worked with Magnet kitchens on all but one of my houses, and despite quite a lot of 'challenges' between us, and a particular branch being utterly useless, we are friends now. Although they often make mistakes, so always check the orders and don't be afraid to complain. Generally, though, I find the service, speed and selection to be good. On the topic of prices, I don't use any Landlord purchasing groups, I've heard they can be great, but I get equal prices (with no membership fee) by going directly to the trade department of suppliers. I buy appliances from Magnet too, unless I want a particular brand for a flip, I've found their prices the best (trust me, I've been around!), I also buy sinks from them. Worktops, however, are expensive here and I usually go elsewhere. For a Flip I would use

Magnet worktops, or an online shop. I have one kitchen from Howdens, but they just can't match the price lately, so despite them having some gorgeous kitchens, it's a no from me. I've tried independents and local showrooms, again they can't match price on the same quality. Negotiation is key, don't accept the first price they give you. Show them other quotes, it's a competitive industry. If you're going to be buying lots of kitchens, then explain this to them so they see the bigger picture and can offer you better deals. Watch them say £10,000 for a kitchen, then the second you haggle, it suddenly becomes £1,997 in an instant. Sounds like Property Training providers…

For bathrooms I've found you can get some bargains online and in the usual physical retailers, but it's all around the same price. With the taps and accessories, it varies a lot, I use any site I can to find the best deals at the time and with a particular style/colour. Local suppliers are also useful for this, especially if your tradespeople get discounts. Tiles can be found cheap anywhere.

For paint, builders get it themselves, usually Dulux for the final coat. However, I have ordered them colour matched paint from Johnstone's which was good, but costly.

Moral of the story; shop around, don't just use my recommendations, you may have your own preferences, and these will change over time and style.

If you don't want to source these things yourself, and you leave it all to the builder, you can't complain when it looks ugly or you don't like it. Either specify exactly what you want to them, or leave it totally to them, e.g. I say I want brushed chrome sockets in the kitchens with black plug holes, not 'get me metal sockets in the kitchen'. They may also add a margin on top for doing this.

I don't source the boring stuff like Plaster, base paint, plasterboards, wires - all the hidden or technical bits.

Snagging
When the builder says it's finished and snagged, ready for tenants. It is not. I promise you.

It's like editing your own work after writing it for hours, you're too involved and your mind is used to what it's seeing, it's much harder to see errors. Your builders have been on site for a long time and their mind will do the same. Now it's your turn to provide feedback, at this point you should be holding 10%+ of the final invoice. I often get a friend who is local and preferably a property investor to go around and give me feedback and evidence (videos/pictures) that I'll share with the builder. This may come at a small cost, or it may be free if there is already a value-exchange (knowledge, contacts etc) but believe me it's a lot cheaper than having a bad property on the market. I have trained people specifically in this aspect, as I'm very fussy and will notice many little errors that will annoy me unless fixed. This can take an hour in each house, which in the grand scheme of things is nothing when you want your house to be finished right.

At this stage or earlier, you want to ensure you have an Electric Safety Certification from a qualified and registered Electrician and a Gas Safe Certification from a registered and qualified gas engineer. The electric cert can cost from £100-250 and the gas £40-100. I've often used the original EPC, however if we've made significant improvements, I will get one for £40-60. Double check that there aren't any more requirements in your local area, things can differ especially if you have landlord licensing in place. Speak to your Letting Agent too about what is required, or the NRLA as it may change from when I wrote this.

Tej Talks

Always take before pictures when you start a project, they will be useful for the refinance stage, I've forgotten to do this multiple times!

Firing a bad builder

I hope you never have to do this, but the reality is you probably will have to, more than once. There is no easy way to do it, simply - it's just communicating they are off the job, for whatever reasons you find. I would take photos, videos and get other quotes too, as evidence if they try and ask for more money. The same goes for bad workmanship, I don't pay for it, simple as that. Evidence here is very useful in supporting your point. Don't take any rubbish from anyone, if it isn't done right - it isn't getting paid for. Also, please take legal action against any cowboy builder you have the displeasure of working with. They should not be getting away with it, it's too easy nowadays and they are horrible. I'm in the process of doing this to 2 'Builders'. Please seek legal advice and look up Money Claims Online.

Keep an eye on the timeframes, daily output and overall attitude of the builders as you progress. If they are lying to you, and clearly not doing the work they are supposed to, get rid of them sooner rather than later. I've waited too long before and it cost me months of opportunity, interest payments and I had a mental breakdown. Some people don't deserve your money or work, so drop them and move on. Your network can support you here, and quickly recommend other builders to rescue a project. This is why it's essential to only pay for work completed correctly, and never let the builder have more money in their pocket, then what's owed.

Keep a list of bad tradespeople, I have one. It's not just my own, but it also has names that have been given to me by other Investors who have had terrible experiences.

Tej Talks

Protect yourself.

I've heard a theory that every Builder has an expiry date, and eventually their speed, quality and attitude will get to the point that you can't stand them anymore. I see some validity in this, unfortunately. Just a theory!

REFINANCE

let's get your money back

REFINANCE

This is how you 'recycle' the initial money you put in. This allows you to pay your investors back and/or buy more houses with the same initial outlay. You also get your house onto a long term, lower interest product compared to bridging or investors, so the real cashflow can come in. This stage is largely controlled by the previous two, if you've done your due diligence correctly then you should know what the end value is likely to be (if assessed correctly). If the refurbishment has been done to a good standard, then the valuer is going to have a positive impression and mark it as 'better' than comparable properties that have sold within the area.

This is the stage where your broker has a big impact, you are working with them to ascertain the best Lender for your personal situation, the property and your future goals.

You can refinance the next day after purchasing a Property, with the right lenders. There is a '6-month guideline' which the vast majority of Lenders will follow, and only allow Remortgages that long after purchase, however there are a bunch who will do it any time before.

Please note, this may change upon publication of this book, and/or when you read it, so speak to a broker for a real-time update.

I go for no more than 75% LTV max, as I want to eventually pay this down, I also choose interest only as I value cash flow more at this stage. Every time I refinance at the end of a fixed term (2, 5, 10-year fixes), I will aim to pay down some of the capital. I go for 5-year fixes usually.

I've shared the pros and cons on the next page when it comes to timeframes on refinances.

PRE 6 MONTHS	POST 6 MONTHS
PROS	
Recycle your cash quickly, pay Investors back and/or carry on purchasing	Wider choice of Lenders and products
Get off a bridge or Investor finance quicker, so less interest to pay	Wider range of interest rates, so you could save money
Buy more properties in less time, with the same initial cash pot	Potentially lower fees and costs
Increase your cash flow, by having smaller monthly outgoings on a mortgage	Some lenders less likely to consider your Refurbishment amount and just value on Open Market Value
CONS	
Increased interest rates and sometimes fees	Staying on a bridge or investor finance for longer, so you pay higher interest than a mortgage
Some lenders will value your property on purchase price plus the refurbishment cost, not the real value	Restricts the speed at which you grow, and the number of properties you can purchase in a given time frame
Less lenders and products available and often less promotional deals	

Tej Talks

You should engage your broker at the start of your business in general, but about 4 weeks from physical completion of a property I would send them all the details of this property. Realistically it shouldn't take more than 1 week to submit your case and book in a valuation, but just open the conversation earlier, as some lenders are based in 1980, and work like snails and love a fax machine. But they may be the best for your situation, annoyingly. If the physical completion is delayed once a valuation is booked, you can always reschedule with no issue.

Choosing a lender
Your decision *may* be fairly limited based on your circumstances, and how soon you are re-mortgaging, but I'll tell you what I look for in a lender and also some of the profiles they will lend to.

I look for lenders that are flexible with their underwriting* policy who will assess each case of its own merits, not off a rigid checklist. I like lenders who are backed by or are Banks, as their funding lines can be stronger and bigger therefore protecting you in a financial crisis. When they have fair upfront fees and a good rate (your broker can compare) I'm more inclined to use them, at the end of the day their customer service is not going to be a primary concern as you'll rarely speak to them. So, price matters above most factors for me.

If you have; bad credit, no salary, no job, no experience, no Residential property, no previous investment property or even a combination of these, you can still get a mortgage. The rate, fees and terms may be less favourable, but it is possible, and your broker will confirm how it may work in your scenario, as many factors are involved.

*(Underwriting is the process of reviewing case information and supporting documentation in line with specific lending policy, in order to make a decision to lend, ask for more information or decline.)

The process
The overall stages and timelines I've worked to are:
1. Broker submits case to lender
2. Lender approves and moves to valuation stage [7 days]
3. Valuation takes place [7 days]
4. Valuer submits report to the lender [1-7 days]
5. Lender officially offers you a mortgage and sends you documents to sign [2-7 days]
6. Your solicitor starts and completes the process [7-28 days]
7. Remortgage funds are sent to you [2-5 days]

From submission to remortgage funds in your account I would factor at least 28 days if your lender and solicitor are shit hot, but it will likely be longer.

These are my timelines that I push, and have worked with a few select Lenders on, however this can vary greatly. Expect last minute document requests from lenders, especially on your first one. Your solicitor will require certain documents from you, I send these the second the remortgage offer lands in their inbox. It means no excuses for delays; I'm not messing around!

That list would be pretty helpful, right?

Here we go:
- AST if it's already let
- Buildings insurance with the 'sum covered'/'reinstatement value' to match the surveyor's value, also to 'note the Lenders interest'
- EPC certificate
- Gas Safe certificate
- Electrical certificate

Tej Talks

- Any works that required Building regulations sign off
- Solicitor's forms regarding the Property and your bank details for left-over funds
- Any necessary landlord licensing registration details (area dependant)
- Your ID and proof of address

If this is coming off a bridge or investor loan, your solicitor will need an updated Redemption Statement. Your Investor can create one easily but bridgers can sometimes take a while to send these over, so email them directly to get it, if the solicitor is being ignored.

Costs

The main costs with a remortgage are your broker, legal, application and valuation Fees. These are costs that must be paid, they can't always be added to the loan like with the lender's administration fee or whatever name it's given. What I mean by 'added to the total loan' is, they essentially loan you the money to then instantly pay their fee. So, you're paying interest on it, and your total loan increases a bit, so when you redeem it, you will actually pay that fee back as opposed to doing it at the start, upfront. With your solicitors, see if they can 'dual represent', meaning they act for the lender and you, this will save you unnecessary cost and time. It means you don't need to use the Lenders in-house or panel solicitors. Their fees are sometimes fixed by the lender and are non-negotiable. On average you'll pay about £350+ for the broker, £550+ for legals, £150+ for application and £250+ for valuation fees. Usually the application fee is non-refundable alongside the valuation fee if it did not happen or was cancelled, however please check this with a broker.

Also, once you're on the mortgage, be aware the first payment is usually higher than the norm because they Pro-Rata it to suit themselves, review the paperwork to understand the breakdown.

Property valuations

In order to prepare for a revaluation, I advise the following:
- Refurbishment completely finished, no signs of damp, damage or cracks
- House cleaned throughout by cleaners, not the Builder
- If it's winter, stick the heating on, if it's Summer then open windows
- Use plug-in air fresheners if it smells like a building site (although I think plaster and paint smell nice!)
- Have a valuation pack prepared for the Surveyor (frankly, I think they just discard these on single lets, but every little helps)
- Be on site with them or have a property investor friend take your place

When the survey is taking place:
- Arrive before the surveyor, be punctual
- Be polite and friendly and show your personality
- Gauge what kind of person they are and adapt your vibe
- Don't tell them how to do their job or what you think the value is
- Expect it to last 5 to 20 minutes
- Hand them the valuation pack at the end, don't say you've added comparable, just say you've prepared something with before/after pictures, details of the refurb etc and hopefully it helps them

Tej Talks

- Depending on their attitude, I'll ask cheekily at the end what they think it's going to be worth, most give an indication, don't believe a word they say until you see the physical valuation

I've gone through a valuation in line-by-line detail on my eLearning Platform, I can't fit all of that detail into this book but I want to go through the core things a valuer is looking for from the valuation documents I have been given, multiple times here.

Valuers are assessing some really basic things like the type of construction, location, date built, if it has any major issues, if it is in a rentable condition, if it's a house or flat, if the roof is flat or pitched and many other questions that we don't have control over.

The key points they are reviewing to assess the value are; size of property and general condition (newly refurbished or dated etc.). You could argue there is the intangible factor of how the property makes them feel, if it's finished to a high standard and dressed well, and it looks the part, perhaps they will increase the value. Just like a potential buyer may increase their offer. However, I prefer to deal with tangibles, and go off what every Surveyor has told me when I've spoken to them in depth.

Size matters.

Dress it up as much as you like, use expensive paint and kitchens but if your house is very small, and all the comparable are larger than yours you may have an issue. Example: Your house is 100sqm, all comparable data is 150sqm and at £150,000, do you think you can reach the same RICS valuation, or even sell for the same? Perhaps, if yours is miles better, but we have to assess this rationally and use data, like a Surveyor should.

That's why it's important to do your research thoroughly beforehand. Having said this, I have been valued at the same as houses which were say 5 to 15 sqm bigger than mine, because it was in A1 condition, so there is some wiggle room, but just be careful with comparable data. When you're first buying it and doing your research, compare the sizes too. I appealed a valuation once, and it got rejected because they had strong evidence *(in their opinion)* which was the same size as my property, despite mine being brand new and shiny. It really feels like a dark art, if it sounds confusing… it is!

I don't think you will ever win an appeal; it makes the surveyor look bad and the lender may reconsider their contract with them, also, hurts the surveyor's ego. I think it's one false corrupt BS system to appeal here.

A buyer is more likely to pay more for a Flip with higher end fixtures than a valuer is to value higher off the same features. So, even more reason to not go overboard on the refurbishment.

I have had a mixed experience with valuers, I've had many who are spot on, but I've had a few who are simply incompetent and unskilled, despite their shiny "RICS" badge. Sorry valuers, love you really xoxo

[CASE STUDY 5] – 82NR

This was actually the first property I ever purchased. A tidy house with not much work required, the Sourcer I used was terrible at managing the project and his builder was rubbish, so this refurbishment cost more than it should have and took longer. The tenant here is really nice and pays above market rent. It is in an area most would say feels a little rough, but it's desirable still. This has been very passive, I did have to spend £750 on fixing part of the roof and guttering, because the sourcer 'doesn't look at the roof or guttering' as part of their fee. There are many reasons I don't need or work with Sourcers, but this taught me a lot and was very insightful. I learnt to be way more detailed in my refurbishments, seek multiple quotes and be pushier with trades. In the sense that I accepted less excuse and expected more work done, and I learnt more about the pricing of different aspects.

I waited 6 months to revalue this because it made the most sense financially as the refurbishment and letting out took a few months and the rates and fees were much better post 6 months. It came in exactly what my research had suggested it should. This was going to be a Bridge purchase with my own money, but the broker who I don't speak to anymore messed that up, so a family member loaned me money. It became a cash purchase, unencumbered, and I used it to Capital Raise to fund my second Property with none of my own money. I have covered that in the Fund It section of the book.

Tej Talks

Purchase Price: £50,000
Stamp Duty (SDLT): £1,500
Sourcing & PM Fee: £5,000
Conveyancing Fee: £550
Refurbishment: £6,500
Interest on Finance: £0

Total money in: £63,617

RICS Valuation: £80,000

Remortgage Amount (75% LTV): £60,000

Money left in*: £3,617

<u>Monthly</u>
Rent: £525
Mortgage Cost: £170
Insurance Cost: £18
Cash flow/Profit: £337

Annual Cashflow/Profit: £3,760
ROCLI: 104%

Tej Talks

RENT

cashflow creation

RENT

Although this is the last part of the model, it is likely to come before the refinance and right after refurbishment, but logically I will place it here. This is a stage that can make or break the next 1, 5, 10 years and beyond. This is where you find the person who is going to pay the rent, every month, for years to come. It's important this stage is taken seriously and not rushed. Tenants have so much, arguably too much protection when they don't pay rent or abide by agreed terms, so you need to be so careful.

I use Letting Agents to find my tenants, as it's time consuming and a lot of admin, I also used to do a similar role in Recruitment, and I don't want to do it again. Also, local agents may know the community and be familiar with people. They offer an understanding of the tenant type and a 6th sense honed throughout their time in lettings for bad tenants. Most will charge the first month's rent to do this, especially since the tenant fee ban (2019) eroded some of their profit. Expect it to take anywhere from 1-14 days to find a good tenant, then another week of referencing and checking, to having the deposit paid ready for their move-in. I've given you a wide time frame because you may list the property slightly higher than the market norm to start with, then reduce it. I've also found that nice homes in 'slower' areas will take longer, especially if you're pushing for a higher rent. Speak to your agent about what's realistic in your area, your properties should be to a good standard, so I'd be aiming for the upper end of the price range, always.

If you don't want to use letting agents to find tenants, you can use websites like Gumtree, OpenRent and others to list and reference yourself. However, Agents may have 'warm' tenants on their database and local knowledge that you may lack, which can mean a quicker tenant find.

Choosing an agent

I have worked with a few great agents, and a few terrible ones. It's not always easy or clear who is good, sometimes you have to work with them to see their true colours come out. As with a lot of things, I go with my gut feeling, especially when deciding between multiple companies.

Here's a list of what I look for and prefer:

- Client money protection, Deposit Protection and registered with a redress scheme *(Wales, Scotland and England may differ in regulation)*
- Polite, warm and clear in their communication
- Good, well taken and lit, photos on their adverts
- Well written adverts using keywords
- Lots of previous adverts changed to 'let' online, meaning they're finding tenants
- Intelligent staff
- Knowledgeable about rental figures, trends and the local market
- I prefer independent smaller agencies to corporates/chains
- It's nice to let the agent who found you a deal, rent it, if they have lettings, but I don't always do this
- Once engaged, I get regular updates and see results quickly. Fire fast if not

Something most Property Investors don't do, is think like a Tech start-up, who would carefully consider their 'CX' or Customer Experience. I want you all to consider your 'TX' Tenant eXperience. The journey they go through from finding an advert online, to getting the keys to their new home and of course the duration of their stay. Your agent is responsible for the first impression and stage of your TX, so make sure they get it right, you want to start how you wish to continue.

You will speak to some agents who will be clueless and use generic all-encompassing terms to convince you that they know what they are doing. Next please! Don't deal with people like this. Either ask for someone else or move onto the next agency. Sometimes I ask what would happen if we listed it really high and see if they respond with honesty or encourage the unrealistic price. I know the tenant types in my areas already, but I will play dumb and look for their honesty on those too. Inquire as to how they vet tenants and what questions they ask them.

If they are going to manage your property, I'd question how many properties they let per month, how many are on their management books and what their default rate is on rental payments. Ask how they deal with arrears; evictions and the things people don't want to discuss. Ask them what justifies their monthly management rate and who their trusted team of tradespeople is, and how long they've worked together. See if they have a standard set of 'call out fees' for their plumber, handyperson etc. Make sure these aren't silly prices.

I also like to look at their reviews online, taking into account the number of them, ratings and any comments made. I ignore industry awards as I don't think they are always honestly judged, and I've had bad experiences with winners of these awards.

When I engage them on a 'Let-Only' or tenant find only basis I expect the following to be done by them:
1. Advertising and marketing
2. Tenant vetting and rejection
3. Referencing and checks

4. House inventory (full colour pictures)
5. Create the AST (tenancy agreement)
6. Process deposit correctly
7. Take first month's rent
8. Serve the AST and required documents on move-in
9. Paint a good picture of me as a landlord, my understanding and flexibility, my passion for property and design
10. Manage tenant expectations – pets, hanging pictures, painting, garden etc.

Full management would include the above, and dealing with any and all monthly issues, collecting rent and chasing arrears.

Choosing a Tenant

I have a basic criterion that I look at across most of my Properties, which is:

- Stable, reliable means to consistently be able to afford the rent
- Combined income above the minimum threshold/affordability level
- Polite and respectful person
- Clean credit scores with no unsatisfied CCJs or any serious CCJs
- Previous renting history with good references

I like to ask the agent what they were like on the viewing, how they came across and what questions they asked, and what their gut feeling is. The referencing and checks will confirm a lot of the information above, but your agent should be asking these before paying for the checks. Don't rush into this, I've done 3 sets of 10 viewings, because I was not 100% on the first 5 offers, I had. I will wait, because this tenant is going to be here for a long time, paying rent every month, so I can wait if I need, for the longer-term benefit. I also request a full credit report.

I know rental demand is high, so I am specific about my ideal tenant, and I will wait longer if I must, to find the right people. I have had houses go on the first day, and others go a few weeks later, and/or with a different agent.

When a new tenancy is started, you or the agent must serve the correct documents in the right manner, failure to do so will cause major issues later down the line if you need to evict the tenant or face legal issues. Check the NRLA for the list of documents and information, this may differ in England, Scotland and Wales. The core items can be; Gas Safe Certificate, EPC Certificate, Confirmation of Deposit Protection, How to Rent Guide and a GDPR Privacy notice. You should ask for written confirmation from your agent that this has been done, you are responsible so make sure the agent is serving documents correctly. The NRLA is priceless, use my code to save money: WHW-000.

Your agent should witness this, but also have a document the tenant signs to confirm they have received all the documents correctly, as evidence.

There are arguments for and against this - but I like to leave a little welcome pack for the tenant, just a small hamper with some chocolates and stuff with a card welcoming them to their new home. It's just a nice touch, don't go all out and put in Champagne and Caviar though… well, unless your house is in Chelsea, darling.

Self-manage Vs agent manage
I think there are two distinct camps here: manage yourself and save a lot of money, with not much actual work most of the time. Or, Agents

manage it and you are totally hands-off and focus on buying more and making more money.

I self-manage, even from 170 miles away. The beauty of single lets is that the management is not intensive, if there's issues with the house then we did not do the refurbishment correctly and the original builder will fix it (or at least *should*). This is why it's important to do that stage correctly, and to spend a little bit more to protect your investment long-term. I also find letting agent's Tradespeople are always more expensive than mine. Plus, I've built up good relationships with mine, so I always want to give them any work I get. With my local network too, I can find help quickly and at a fair price. Therefore, using an agent makes no sense as I'm organising everything anyway. Most months (excluding during COVID-19) I spend very little time on my houses that are already tenanted, and the rent flows in.

Tenant relationships - I have good ones with all of them, yes potentially they may take it more seriously if an agent is involved, but I find them an inconvenient middleperson generally.

How passive have my BTLs been? Very, the most work I've had to put in over since the start has been issuing a new AST (admin work) and working with tenants through Coronavirus and losing jobs, but both did not take long and most were done on my phone. As I grow, I will consider setting up my own lettings agency to manage my properties, at the moment I've designed an in-house function to be run by VAs, who will respond to tenants and tradespeople, coordinating everything happening with my overwatch. This means I will be more hands-off, but still aware of what's happening.

I've got a table comparing both in my opinion, on the next page.

SELF-MANAGE	AGENT
An extra 10 – 15% a month income. Annually this becomes a significant chunk	Peace of mind that someone locally should be looking after your investment
More personal relationships with tenants, meaning potentially more influence during challenges	Barrier between you and tenants if things get tricky, a mediator of sorts
Tenancy law can be complex, and you need to understand it. You should use the NRLA to support you	Agents have to understand tenancies and should be experienced in handling issues and serving documents correctly
You may require licensing or to be part of a paid scheme	Locally based, so they could react to issues quicker than you
In single lets, if the tenant is chosen well, there should not be much work to do monthly	They have insurances and redress schemes to ensure they behave and you can complain

Ensure that regular inspections are carried out, I set the first one at 3 months from move in, then 6 months after that. I will get a professional company to do one or ask my local friends.

I won't cover dealing with issues that arise with tenants, as various landlord bodies cover this and can offer advice at a very low cost. I will say, if you are self-managing then it's nice to check in with tenants every now and then, especially in tough economic times or a pandemic. I would consider sending them birthday cards too, think about TX. Yes, you need to maintain professionalism and not take excuses for lack of rental payments etc, but why not be different to almost every other Investor?

With arrears, when self-managing I think you need to be firm if these issues arise. First, please communicate with the tenant and try to understand the reasons behind this, Coronavirus for example, was tough on everyone, don't just assume they are bad people.

Remove the inevitable emotions and handle it appropriately. Always send reminders multiple times, do not harass them however and always stay well within the laws. Create systems to automatically remind tenants, even if a payment plan is agreed. They need to know you are not a pushover, and arrears are serious. It's incredibly frustrating when they don't take it seriously. All that hard work you put into creating a beautiful home for them, the others you turned away, for them to be ungrateful to this extent and often to behave in such a horrible way. It's easy to take it personally, trust me, I feel your pain. The system is shit; landlords are treated like crap, even though we create homes for people and add high quality stock to the market.

SCALING
QUICKLY

explosive growth is painful

Because I've purchased 15 houses in 9 months using very little of my own money, I want to deliver some more sauce in the form of some additional principles. I recall many months ago I just wanted to buy 3 in a year, and I'd be happy. Things clearly changed!

You're on your own path, so you do what works for you, you don't need to grow quick. There is a lot of pain and discomfort that comes with these achievements. There are no secrets, working hard and smart is what pays off. Growing quickly has been one of the most stressful, anxious and frustrating periods of my entire life. But, it's worth it for me in the end. Well, that's what I tell myself anyway.

Remember, with speed comes mistakes, and with growth comes hurt.

People before Profits

I live by this, honestly money is great, and it lets you live the life you want to, how else will I afford a Calcutta Marble castle? But really, I don't give a shit about it. Seriously, every house I buy I don't think 'oh great another £350 a month'. I think about the kitchen, bathroom and swag, about how I get to do what I'm so passionate about and create a wonderful home. That's my motivation. As simple as it sounds, if you are solely driven by money, then this will be a sad lonely path you're embarking on. I've been there, we all have something we truly care about, or someone. Go back to the start of the book and think about your why.

We have to realise that people will make or break our business. We are not doing every step of this process, an expert is (solicitor, broker, builder etc) so our relationships with them are vital. Nothing talks louder than action, and once you buy more houses, give your teams more work - it elevates you to a different category in their client list. Prices and service will reflect this. Be good to people, do the right thing and communicate properly. I've lost relationships and money because of poor communication; I've learnt the hard way. If someone does well by you, then trust them (to an extent) because trust is needed to ensure a smooth relationship and more efficient process. With the tips in this book, I feel you will be somewhat protected from people breaking your trust, but when it happens - fix the problem, and move on.

Consistency is key
You need to be following up every single viewing, offer, conversation, rejection. Set timers in your diaries or CRMs, whatever, just make sure it happens. Have KPIs for following up, it takes multiple touch points to form a relationship, make a sale or secure a deal. Don't give up, don't look at others doing it with ease and complain. That will be you shortly, with the right work ethic. I follow up like a bulldog, I'm very persistent. This has allowed me to access deals that others forgot about, or only ever viewed once then never mentioned them again. Having a good memory helps with this, I can remember almost every house I viewed when I see a trigger (road name, picture etc.).

Money
You need money to grow quickly, and an abundance of it. Builders invoices will hit you quickly, as will monthly interest payments, investor repayment and the other costs with property. Ensure you have worked out all your costs beforehand, and where possible have Investors lined up to invest, or you already have the funds. You will find deals, but you need to be able to actually purchase them, and have funds ready to show agents and vendors, so that they take you seriously. This book doesn't cover raising finance in great detail, as this is focussed on BRR itself. Perhaps I'll write another one purely based on Investor finance, as I have raised £598,000 in a few months. However, my branding tips at the start are a key element to this and I have a module on it, on my eLearning platform.

Tej Talks

I'm always learning and sharing insight into my progress on my podcast, so you'll find a lot of information there too.

I would have grown quicker, if I grew slower.

I've made a lot of mistakes. I've lost so much profit, I've had to sell properties I wanted to keep and vice versa. It's been incredibly stressful, and I've been very unhappy, and had breakdowns throughout this journey. I've dealt with idiots almost every day, and still do. I'm grateful to my investors who gave me a chance so early on. The pain is real, and would I recommend buying 15 properties in 9 months from a standing start? Not really. Is the end goal as 'passive' and worth it, as people make out? I think so. Please take it from me, protect your physical and mental health from day one. Set boundaries, set a structure, look after yourself.

I've struggled a lot mentally and it can really get you down. Not once have I considered giving up. I can't. I see things through no matter the pain, it's not weak to give up, sometimes you have to, sometimes you have to breakdown to rebuild stronger again. If you're feeling overwhelmed, tired, struggling, angry, upset, attacked or helpless, if it helps, I've been there. I feel you.

I really hope this book has given you insight into the reality of property, the issues, challenges and rewards. My mistakes serve as lessons for you, and I hope they always will.

INSIGHT FROM MY SQUAD

bonus section

Shaz Ahmed, Finance Broker

Your broker is an essential part of your team. But it's all for nothing if you're not working together, on the same page, towards the same goal. As a broker I work primarily with property investors at different stages of their journeys and varying experience – but the principals and processes are pretty much the same.

Basic documents

Straight away I would encourage you to get the following documents ready to send to your broker and ensure they're up to date and still valid.

- Photo ID – passport or driving license
- Proof of Address – latest Council Tax letter or recent utility bill
- Proof of Income – 3 months latest payslips or if self-employed 2 years latest SA302s / Tax Calculations with corresponding Tax Year Overviews

Ensure your proof of funds are watertight

If you get this right on day one you won't go far wrong. For bridging projects, typically, lenders are fine with funds from 3rd party sources via gifts or loan agreements. But they'll need sight of a gifted deposit letter or the loan agreement itself and may even ask for proof of funds (being in the account for 6 months) in the 3rd party's account. If you're using your own money, again get your bank statements ready to show that you've held the money for a certain period of time.

You may also need evidence that you have enough in the bank for the refurbishment plus contingency. If your bridging lender is funding the refurbishment, this is usually via drawdowns, so you'll need enough to kickstart the project. In short, have the documentation ready so that your source of funds for deposit and refurbishment is crystal clear.

Having robust Proof of funds also gives the lender that you're a serious proceedable investor and not just looking for quotes.

Schedule of Works

This is a very important document for any BRR project. Ask your broker for a template although the lender will normally have their own variation. The SOW should itemise the work that will be carried out on the property and specify the length of time needed for each element and the cost. The surveyor gets given a copy and will comment on it as part of their report. It also helps the lender – if they are funding the work – determine the drawdown schedule.

The Schedule of Works needs to be timely, costed appropriately and value adding to the property in question

Invest in a scanner

You're a property investor, right? Then invest in the right tools for your business. You will need to send a minimum set of documents to the lender – via the broker – for any application you do. And, it's no good if you send photos of your hands, your lovely oak table or anything else other than the document itself! Ideally it will need to be high quality PDF scans. At worst, a clear scan with an app like Cam Scanner (other apps are available) will do.

Get to know your credit file

Your credit profile is your Financial Passport. It tells lenders where you've been and where you're likely to end up in the future. Keep on top of it as there can be occasional inaccuracies and entries that need correcting. Lenders will commonly use either Experian, Equifax or TransUnion.

Nothing else will do!

Tell your broker everything

There's nothing worse than an underwriter coming back and saying, *"Can you explain the missed credit card payment from 5 months ago?".*

Specialist lending, and one of the purposes of using a broker, is all to do with positioning and credibility. All of that goes to pot when the underwriter brings up something that should have been disclosed and explained from day one. So, one more time for those at the back – "Tell your broker everything and trust them to position you appropriately."

Be ready to pay fees

One of the reasons to apply for a bridging loan is for the speed element, right? Well, nothing is going to happen until you pay your fees. Typically, the upfront costs will be valuation, lenders legal and broker fees. Some lenders may also charge an administration fee upfront. The broker will likely not submit the case until their fees are paid & the lender will not instruct the survey or their legal team until they have been paid.

Once you have your initial bridging loan your broker should be keeping in touch to see how the project is coming along but either way let them know when you are ready for the property to be refinance onto a mortgage. Communication is key throughout the process.

As the old saying goes, teamwork makes the dream work.

I have worked with Shaz on 10+ deals. He is an amazing broker with 10 years' experience, very responsive and knowledgeable. He's active on social media, a regular networker, public speaker and all-round finance superstar. He also knows the best places to eat. I trust no one else with my Mortgages. **@WheresShaz**

Pinder Dariwal - Falcon Insurance:

Property insurance is something every property owner should have, but what exactly is it and why is it so important? Here we will answer all your property insurance related questions, and all the questions you never even thought to ask.

What is property insurance, and does it actually work?

In its most basic terms, property insurance is a range of policies that provide property owners with protection and liability coverage. It involves the owner paying a set sum regularly, usually monthly, for which they will receive a financial reimbursement if there is any damage or theft to the property, and to cover third-parties' injuries on the property.

Property insurance is available from a number of different companies and everyone will greatly vary in what they offer and how much they cost. The insurance offered by different companies usually includes a range of policies and not all insurance policies will cover your property for every eventuality. People often question whether insurance actually works and if it is worth paying for. There have been cases where property owners have been unable to claim and/or haven't been covered for their damages/theft/injuries. Of course, these individuals then feel disgruntled that they've paid for insurance for years but haven't been given help when they needed it. In these cases, the problem is often in the insurance policy and the fact that they haven't made sure it is comprehensive enough to cover them in every instance.

Tej Talks

It is important to shop around, understand the insurance policies in detail and make sure the policy you choose to take out covers everything you might need it to.

What are the risks of not having property insurance?
Property insurance is highly recommended because there are serious risks involved with not having a good insurance policy in place. Your property can get damaged, it can be a target for theft, or someone could injure themselves whilst on your property. If you do not have insurance in place to cover you in these eventualities, then you are taking a risk.

These risks include:
- Loss of revenue (if the property is rented out or used for business)
- An inability to afford repairs or replacement of anything damaged or stolen
- An inability to afford compensation claims
- Legal action being taken against you personally in the event of someone injuring themselves on your property
- Legal action prompted by you for damages/thefts to your property caused by a third party
- Finance Lenders will require you to insure the property, to protect their security

If you have property insurance in place and the policies cover you properly, you do not have any of the risks above, the insurance company assumes full responsibility.

How to choose a good insurance product

Before you begin looking at insurance policies, take some time to consider what it is you want from your policy. What do you want it to include? What do you need to be covered for? And what is the property being used for? Also, what is your insurance budget? The answers to these questions will help you to narrow down the wide selection of insurance policies available, helping you to choose the perfect policy for your property. *(Tej: This is where a good broker makes your life way easier)*

Once you have an idea what you need from an insurance policy, start researching the ones available. Select the best policies to create a shortlist, and then look at the following:

- What does the policy include? Does it cover you for everything you need it to?
- What fees are involved with making a claim? If the excess on the policy is very high, you might find that although you *can* claim, it is actually cheaper not too
- Check if there is a limit as to what you can claim. Some policies will not only charge you a fee for claiming, but they will also limit the amount you can claim. This can be a problem if something major happens to your property and it will be costly to repair
- Is the company a reputable company? The last thing you want when you have to claim on your insurance, is to find that the insurance company is no longer operational or is unable to support your claim. Dealing with a reputable insurance company that has been established for years, will give you peace of mind

Tej Talks

What does the insurance jargon actually mean?

When you read through the terms and conditions of your insurance, you'll be faced with a lot of specialist terms that you might not be familiar with. Here are some of the most commonly used with explanations.

- Accidental damage cover: This covers accidental damage to your property. The insurance will replace or repair accidental damages caused.

- Act of God: This is a clause usually found in insurance documents where 'acts of God' or 'acts of war' are excluded, therefore not covered by the insurance. Acts of God include natural disasters, such as flood.

- All-risks: Some insurance policies cover all risks and will note any exclusions. If your insurance policy notes 'all-risks' check to make sure there are no exclusions.

- Annual policy: This is an insurance policy that lasts for the term of a year.

- Broker: This is an independent intermediary that sells different policies from a number of insurance companies. By law, they must be registered.

- Buildings insurance: This insurance covers the building only, against things like floods and fires.

- Contents insurance: This insurance covers the possessions within your property, although it doesn't always cover everything.

- Excess: This is the amount you will have to pay the insurance company when you make a claim.

- Exclusions: These are things that are not covered by your insurance policy.

- Indemnity: This is a principle within the insurance policy which guarantees the policy holder that if they suffer damage/theft, the insurance company will make sure they are put back into the same financial position as they were before the problem occurred.

- Insurance Premium Tax (IPT): This is government tax which is charged as a percentage of insurance premiums.
- Legal expenses insurance: Covers the costs of any private legal action.
- Loss adjuster: The specialist who deals with large and/or complicated insurance claims.
- Loss Assessor: The person that negotiates claims for the policyholder.
- Material fact: This is information that affects whether an insurance company will accept a policy, and the premium it would charge.
- New-For-Old: Also called 'replacement as new', this is where an insurance company guarantees to replace something that is lost or broken, for a brand-new item, without deducting anything for wear and tear.
- Policyholder: This is the person that takes out the policy.
- Premium: The regular charge a customer pays for their insurance cover.
- Public Liability Policy: Covers any legal liability associated with injury and damage to third parties.
- Settlement: This is when the insurer pays a claim.
- Under-insurance: When a customer hasn't taken out the correct level of insurance and have been paying less than they should.
- Underwriter: This is someone who decides whether to accept a risk and also calculates the premium.

Different types of property insurance

The property insurance you need will greatly depend on what you are using the property for. For this reason, there are a number of different property insurance types available.

These include:
- Buy-To-Let (BTL): insurance for properties that are bought with the purpose of renting them out as an income.
- FLIP: insurance for properties that are brought with the view of refurbishing and rebuilding them to re-sell at a higher cost.
- Serviced Accommodation (SA): insurance for properties that will be rented, fully furnished, on a short or long-term basis.

Is rent guarantee worthwhile?

Rent guarantee is worthwhile, especially if you are a landlord reliant on the regular income from rent in order to pay your mortgage on the property. Rent guarantee covers your monthly rental costs if your tenant is unable to pay. This is something some policies include, but not all, so if this is something you need you should make sure it is included.

Rental arrears can have a massive impact upon your finances as the property owner. When a tenant defaults on their rent it can be months before you are able to recover your money and, in that time, you will have to pay any costs for the property (such as the mortgage) yourself. For this reason, rent guarantee is worth it for the peace of mind it provides.

Industry veteran Pinder Dhaliwal is the CEO of Falcon Insurance, a Birmingham based award winning commercial insurance broker. Falcon insurance has committed to delivering the right insurance for each of their clients.

"Price should not be your benchmark of Quality" our team works extremely hard to make sure that all of our clients have a policy that suits their unique needs. So, whether you're in construction, engineering, manufacturing, property or need Professional Indemnity cover Falcon Insurance will have a solution to fit your needs

0121 679 7265
enquiries@falconinsurance.co.uk

I work with the team at Falcon Insurance on all my properties and it's a breeze, and I'm grateful they put together so much information for us. They are based in the Jewellery Quarter in Birmingham but operate nationally.

Tej Talks

Paul Weller - Astonia Associates

Buying property is great, so is the income, but you want to run an efficient and profitable business that makes the most of your allowances and minimises your tax liability. This is just a snapshot from Paul my Accountant. Please seek out proper personalised advice from an Accountant or Tax specialist like him. This is not financial advice.

Extracting profit from your Ltd company:

- Operating through a limited company gives directors/shareholders flexibility as to when they extract profits.
- They can use a combination of salaries and dividends and can also 'time' in which tax year certain profits are extracted in order to save tax.
- Other family members who are genuinely working in the business can be included as directors/shareholders or employed in the business in order to potentially use their tax allowances and tax bands.
- Post corporation tax profits can be left in the limited company to build the property portfolio, which is a tax efficient way of saving for deposits for future purchases.
- Each person has a £2,000 a year tax free allowance to receive dividends so this can be utilised where possible.
- And directors/shareholders can also charge interest on the loans they put into the company if that is appropriate too.

What can be claimed as a cost against your profits:
'Capital expenditure' cannot be deducted in computing the profits of a property business.

Examples of capital expenses include:
- Expenditure which adds to or improves the land or property; for example, converting a disused barn to a holiday home
- Expenditure on extensions
- Other major improvements

Care also needs to be taken with the cost of refurbishing or repairing a property purchased in a derelict or run-down state. In these cases, the costs incurred in bringing the property into use for the first time will be considered as capital and not 'revenue'. This contrasts with such costs incurred by a landlord on a property owned and previously rented out for many years where they would be treated as 'revenue'. This is not always a clear-cut situation, and will depend on the specific circumstances, so it will be important to get advice in advance.

If you are carrying out a refurbishment project, the first question to ask is whether any of the expenditure would qualify as a repair. The repair must be a 'like for like' replacement of an existing asset (e.g. a replacement boiler, replacement windows or replacement concrete floor etc). If this is the case, then it is likely that 100% tax relief would be available for the expenditure incurred.

However, if any part of the refurbishment is an improvement as opposed to a repair then this will be treated as capital expenditure. Capital expenditure on the structure of the building (e.g. walls, floors, ceilings etc) will not attract any tax relief. However, capital allowances may be available if any of the expenditure is for Plant and Machinery (P&M) or Integral Fixtures and Fittings (IFF).

BRR expenses can be a complicated area depending upon the size of the property and also whether items are being replaced or improved, so seeking advice is always recommended as It is largely a question of fact and degree in each case whether expenditure on a property leads to an improvement.

- Generally replacing the kitchen and bathroom suites are allowable if they are like-for-like replacements (same number of cupboards etc). Generally, these items would be allowed to be offset against your property profits
- If you decorate your property then you will be able to claim 100% of the costs and the same applies to the replacement of curtains, carpets and furniture
- There is an HMRC website (*Search Property Income Manuals PIM2030*) for all the detail - says that alterations due to advancements in technology are generally treated as an allowable repair rather than an improvement. So, as an example, when single glazed windows are replaced with double glazing this is allowable
- Replacements of boilers, plumbing and wiring are generally allowable and help you to reduce profits and subsequently tax

---

Paul has been running tax and accountancy practices for 20 years, he does all my company accounts and is very helpful for my random queries and curiosity! I shopped around for an Accountant, but Paul was the most sensibly priced and we got on well, plus he has Property Investment experience too. Mention me if you message him.

www.astonia-associates.co.uk
paul@astonia-associates.co.uk - 07887 907080

Stuart Forsdike – PCS Legal

I hope everyone has enjoyed the book so far and gained useful information from Tej regarding property.

Now for the boring part!

Conveyancing explained

Once you have found a property to buy whether it be a house or a flat, there is the legals to take care of. Conveyancing is the legal transfer of title from a seller to a buyer. A conveyancing transaction has two main phases; exchange and completion. Exchange is when you become legally bound to buy (or sell) and completion is the date the property you are buying legally becomes yours.

The legal process of conveyancing is an investigation of the property you are looking to buy. Most buyers focus on whether the property is good value, the potential yield or its structure i.e. is there anything wrong with it. Of equal importance must be the legal process. If the legal process doesn't go to plan, then you may find your buying a headache. It's of upmost importance that what your buying has a good and marketable title. The title must be investigated to ensure its clear of any charges, restrictions or notices. A buyer will also need to be aware of any rights of way, covenants and so on. This is really just the basics!

Any reader of this must note that each property is different in relation to its title. It means what might apply to one might not another. Hopefully the following information will help you when buying in terms of understanding and of course making the legal process quicker and smoother.

ID and AML

Once you have found a property to buy and picked a lawyer – either Solicitor, Legal Executive or Licensed Conveyancer you will need to provide various ID. You may have already supplied this to your broker as covered in this book already or indeed a lender. You will still in addition need to supply not only ID to support who you say you are but also ID relating to your money to satisfy Money Laundering regulations. It's always a good idea to have saved in advance copies of your passports and driving licenses together with bank statements showing the money you will use. You also need to supply your lawyer with further information on how you gained such money. For example, if it's a gift from a relative they will also need to go through the same process. You must do this as soon as you can. Legally, a lawyer should not start to form any business relationship without holding this information.

Freehold or leasehold

There are two main property types being freehold and or leasehold. A freehold property is where you own all of the property/building and leasehold generally only part of it. Although you do get leasehold houses, generally in the UK freehold properties are houses and leasehold properties flats. Whilst buying freehold properties is a simpler process, the same can't be said of a leasehold. A leasehold property is often more complex in its nature due to expanded covenants and rights of way.

With any leasehold property comes a lease. The lease is the document that sets out all the conditions of its ownership and any rules and regulations. The lease document will contain a lease term which is the period of which the lease runs. When this time period runs out, the property will revert to the freeholder. Furthermore, most banks will not lend monies against a leasehold property that has a lease term of 75 years or less. So, if you're thinking about buying leasehold property with a short lease, its highly likely the issue of its term will arise whilst you own the property. If you have such a lease term to contend with then you will need to attend to extending it or purchasing the freehold if possible. Extending the lease terms is known as a lease extension and the document is called a deed of variation. The key point is that a freeholder will charge a fee for extending the term which can vary depending on the length. This can massively vary.

In addition to the lease term you should also consider the amount of Ground Rent you might have to pay. Firstly, is it affordable and does it eat at your profit. Secondly, does it double? Lenders really dislike doubling ground provisions!

Other payments include that of building insurance and also service charge. Service charge is where either the landlord or an appointed managing agent charges a fee relating to how much it costs to maintain the estate. This can go up (or down, but unlikely) depending on many factors.

Finally, you need to consider whether the service charge may increase in the future. The landlord can serve what is called a section 20 notice at any point should any common areas or fixtures need maintenance or repair meaning a big bill could be on its way to you. You certainly don't want to buy a flat to then find out you may be liable for contributing towards the installation of a new lift!

This is not a full list of what to look out for but merely a cross section of common issues. Sometimes, you can find the whole lease has been incorrectly drafted and can be classed as defective and therefore it

Tej Talks

really is important you instruct a property lawyer as early as possible on your journey

Searches

Sometimes there is information registered against the property that is not recorded at land registry. Often searches will reveal these. There are many searches that are property and geographically specific. There isn't room to cover all of them, but the most common and most likely searches required on any property type and in any location are a Local Authority, Drainage, Chancel (depending when the seller brought the property) and Environmental.

A local Authority search will contain any information about the property that is held at the local council. This can be for example, details on planning and building regulations, smoke and tree preservation orders, compulsory purchase orders, grants, and details on roads being public or private. If buying a property on a private road you may as a user have to pay for its upkeep. The local search of course contains far more information that your lawyer will discuss with you when you receive the results. Point to note – it is essential you pay particular attention to the planning register held at the local authority if you're thinking about extending and such work may require planning. You may find this has already been applied for and refused etc.

The drainage search will have vital information on connectivity to both water and foul drainage plus also drain location. Again, important if you are to extend a property. The Environmental search will focus on matters relating to land contamination, subsidence, flooding and radon – just to name a few. Finally, chancel liability is something you may not know about.

The searches will tell you of any potential liability attached to the property that again may affect your enjoyment or importantly any profit you are looking to make.

Time Frames

Clients often ask how long things take – well it maybe a sit on the fence answer, but it really depends on the circumstances of both the buyer and seller but also the property. A property will be simple or complex relating to its title – not it's price, as is commonly thought. A million-pound house may be a lot easier to convey that a £50,000 flat. The flat could therefore take twice as long. An average transaction will take 12-14 weeks to reach exchange of contracts where both parties are legally bound and 14-16 weeks to reach completion when it legally becomes the buyers. This is only an average and should not be relied upon. One thing is for certain, there is no such thing as a simple transaction and whilst you can instruct and even exchange and complete on the same day this applies to certain property only. It's rare to exchange and complete within weeks and any buyer or seller should always prepare for at least the average to manage expectations

Title Documents

Once your offer is accepted and the process moves into legals, a lawyer will assess the title, and advise you on:

Covenants - these are things you must or mustn't do whilst an owner of the property. For example, decorate the outside every 3 years or a covenant that prevents an extension being built.
Easements – these in the main relate to rights of way. I.e. a neighbour could have a legal right over the land a property has been built upon. You don't want to buy where the neighbour can walk their dog through your garden!

Tej Talks

Restrictions – this is something that does what it says on the tin. You must know a restriction can be removed from the title or consent given to remove, as if not you may not be able to register your ownership at land registry and therefore the property is unsellable.

You as a buyer can find out valuable information on the property you're buying. I would always check the seller's full names are contained in the proprietorship register i.e. is the person you're dealing with the seller. You can also check if the seller has any charges on the property and also what they may have paid for it when they purchased. Sometimes covenants will also be detailed in the title giving you a 'heads up' on what your buying with even before the conveyancing.

Auctions
There is a different process for buying a property through auction. When you win a bid on a property at auction you are legally bound straight away, you've exchanged contracts. The very best bit of legal advice I can give anyone buying at auction is simple. Ask your lawyer to help before you bid not after. I have lost track of how many clients have purchased a property that has cost them literally thousands and thousands to sort out. This can range from a breach of planning, sitting tenants, defective leases, the list really and I mean really is endless...

Summary
These are just some of the matters that come up within the conveyancing process. It's a complicated process and one that a property lawyer will aid you with. All lawyers are covered by insurance and as a client you therefore have the upmost protection when looking to buy. Don't try to save money on this part of the process. You're spending significant money on something to live in or for investment. Other subjects and things to consider are lawyer fees, stamp duty, buying as a limited company or in your name. There are many other

Tej Talks

parts of the other process too. Once completion takes place do you know there are further months where notices are served, SDLT submissions are made to the inland revenue and finally registration of the property at the land registry. Take a step back - yes, it's the boring part maybe, but equally whether you're buying to live in or buying for investment you're doing it for an important reason.

Don't underestimate just how important the legal process really is.

I've worked with Stu and the PCS team over 7+ deals now, they are fantastic. He personally has 23 years in the legal field and is a Licensed Conveyancer and Senior Director. He's very responsive and helps me out with all sorts of legal queries... *(I do get into a bit of beef sometimes!)*

I work with them on all my cash purchases and flip sales. If you'd like a quote, please get in touch with them and quote TEJ TALKS:

stuart.f@pcslegal.co.uk

FREQUENTLY ASKED QUESTIONS

cheeky extra value for you

Have you ever Struggled to get finance from a Bridger or Mortgage Lender?

Yes, but because I engaged a broker from early on and sorted my paperwork etc out as early as possible it was a bit easier. I had an issue with affordability on a bridge once, as my cash flow was negative, but they retained more interest upfront instead. However, I've had issues with bad Valuers down valuing me so much that it's below the Lenders 'minimum loan size' so I've been stuck. In fact, I'm stuck right now on two. Keep an eye on my IG for updates.

Should I remortgage my house to get cash to buy Investments with?

This depends on your risk appetite. If you've spent your life paying down your mortgage, do you really want to start it again? If you have a partner and kids, people who rely on this house, then of course the risk is increased. However, you may have huge equity in the house that is sitting there doing nothing. It's an option if you are happy with taking on this extra debt and risk of repossession on the roof above your head. There is no right answer, this is a discussion for you to have with other people who may own the house, and also with yourself. Compare the cost of this finance versus other types too. Your view may change as you invest more, as your risk appetite and attitude towards this kind of debt can change. Seek professional advice.

Will BTLs let me quit my job quickly?

If you have just finished this book, then you know the answer. No! They are a great asset in general, but they are not the quickest way. The actual cash flow per house is not enough to have a significant impact without a larger number of them, which takes time. I believe Rent to Rent is the quickest way to bring in cash flow, learn about property and let you go full time. Deal sourcing is also a fantastic way to start, it teaches you a lot and gets you hands-on experience, but do us all a favour, and be a decent one.

How do you keep your skin so youthful with all the stress?
Well, I have to shout out my momma for that one, big up her genes.
Really, it's a combination of Sanctuary, BodyShop, Clarins and Nivea.
Drinking lots of water and exfoliating regularly, oh and Punjabi spices
like Haldi (turmeric), and Coconut oil.

Should I start a Podcast?
Start with the why, then the execution. Can you commit? Can you
bring something different to the game? Is it really the most efficient
way to build a brand? (in my opinion no) Will you enjoy it? Plenty of
these start every week, but how many last and become firm favourites.

I've written a Podcast guide, 18 pages and 45 minutes of video content,
updated regularly. Check out my guide and make your decision from
there - tej-talks.com/ebooks

Should I pay for Education?
Ah, what a question! Yes and no. This is not a straightforward answer,
because it really depends on your personal situation and goals. I spent
six months networking, buying people Nando's to get an hour with
them, reading every book and listening to every podcast, reading
through groups on Facebook and putting myself out there, before I did
one viewing.

Could I have skipped this period, paid money and got ahead?
Probably. If there was a course that added real value, and went through
all the details, taught by someone who's doing it right now, yes it would
have made a difference. However, it's not easy to find a course like this,
which is why I sometimes teach or mentor people, as I try to deliver
what's missing.

There are endless options, so please leave the credit card at home, separate yourself from the excited atmosphere at free events and make a slow, rational decision. Ask difficult questions, assess someone's Brand, do you want to learn from a Marketer or an Investor? Look past the selling, shouting and emotional manipulation, to the potential value and return on your investment.

Where do you find the time to do so much?

I don't find it, I manage it. I love Branding and using Social Media, so the time I spend on it I don't notice, because it's fun. Same with viewings and refurbishments. Also, my situation allows me to go all out - I'm full time, I live at home, 5 days a week I can work from 8am until 11pm, as I only see my Fiancé for the whole weekend. So, just because you see someone's success online, don't forget we all have unique situations which are a part of our progress or lack of. Use tools that can track your time, block out your calendar, get an accountability partner - take action to make it happen. Hard work pays off, there is no shortcut to success.

BTLs then Flips or which order?

I say both at the same time. If you're starting with a small amount of cash, and you want to multiply it, maybe whilst you work full time. Then, buying BTLs with small increases in cash flow per month is not going to do that. You need to do multiple Flips, generate chunks of cash and build your cash. Yes, you miss out on capital appreciation, but perhaps making the cash pot bigger at the start is a smarter way to then buy multiple BTLs at once, and create the 'passive' cash flow to quit your job? Consider all options and think logically. With Flips you may attract more Investors, who want a shorter loan length, but at a higher interest rate or a profit share. You can afford to do this with Flips because of the profit.

Do you train or mentor?

Not very often, and only with select people. If you'd like to find out more and see if we are a good fit for each other, then please contact me. Also, Check out tej-talks.com/education.

I've also launched an eLearning Experience because this book covers a huge amount, but I want to expand on this. I want to show you things visually, talk through spreadsheets, analyse live deals and more. For the list of what I cover on the eLearning that wouldn't fit in this book:

- Deal Analysis live with the spreadsheet and real portal property, every data field explained
- Using EPCs to understand internal floor size and make your comparables much more accurate
- How to use cash flow spreadsheets with real examples
- Live viewings and virtual tours to highlight issues and costs
- Refurbishments before and after, photos annotated with explanations of work done and cost
- System set up on screen (Project Management Apps and more)
- Case studies of deals and everything that went wrong
- Basic guide to using online portals to find deals and getting vendors details
- Estate agent roleplays
- Online Auctions, tips tricks and using EIG
- Raising finance and how I've borrowed £598,000 plus FCA compliance
- JV Basics
- In Depth Bridging Finance and why it's awesome
- Videos of me snagging properties and comprehensive list
- Interior Design basics with visuals and tricks to save money
- Designing your valuation pack

Tej Talks

Plus, it will cover everything else in the book again too, if you prefer a video/audio format. It's low priced, modular and you can find it here:

www.tejsingh.me

I'm grateful you purchased this book, so I'll give you a cheeky discount, enter the code **TEJBOOK2020.**

I will be joined by well-known guest speakers in the industry throughout the eLearning experience too, sharing their expertise.

If you aren't already, please follow me on:

IG - @tej.talks
FB - The Tej Talks Podcast
YouTube - Tej Talks
LinkedIn - Tej Singh

Join my weekly mailing list at tej-talks.com and my Podcast is available there, or any Podcast app of your choice.

ACKNOWLEDGEMENTS

gracias

Tej Talks

Geena, for supporting me as a person through everything in the last 7 years, being my best friend, and the most genuine and positive influence in my life. Dealing with the breakdowns, the mood swings and the lack of face time with me as I built my business. Truly a superstar and the love of my life. The only person I want to eat salami and cheese with, in an Italian village, off the beaten path, for the rest of my life.

Mum for always supporting me, raising me to be a good person with ethical values in a loving home. She's an amazing woman who has achieved so much in life and handles stress with a real stoic mind. I got my good music taste and dancing skills from her.

Dad for being my biggest fan, watching all my IG Lives and providing me with all my audio-visual equipment. Thanks for all your help, love and keeping my old car on the road despite numerous issues.

Mama Ji, Dada Ji, Nani Ji and Nana Ji for keeping me well fed and trying to fatten me up! But seriously, for looking out for me, in a very overly cautious older generation Punjabi way. Of course, for their raw, savage comments on everything too, hah! I love them for all they have done for me growing up. My Nana Ji taught me how to stay calm, communicate with a smile and was a big influence on me. I miss him every day.

Syme we didn't have the best relationship growing up, throwing apples at each other isn't very fruitful, but I know we are good now. Thanks for your support, laughter and sending me cute cat/dog pics.

Shaz Ahmed for writing the broker part, and for sorting all my mortgages efficiently and responding super quickly. This guy seems to know everything about finance, at any hour of the day, or night. He also proofread the Refinancing part.

Jon Smart for getting my Bridging and remortgages done so quickly, knowing exactly what the lender requires. Plus, lots of legal help when I needed it the most, and a great service.

Stuart Forsdike, Maria Enright and the PCS Team for completing transactions quickly, giving me the best prices and for always offering Legal Guidance and interesting facts!

Katie Melbourne, Zac Zorno at Together Finance. Sorting my bridging all the time with absolute ease and no hassle to me, and always working with me to understand more complex cases.

Pinder Dhaliwal and the Falcon team. I send an address, next thing I know my property insurance is all sorted and in place. As easy as that.

Cate Brooks for doing viewings for me, snagging properties, being my ear to the ground and just being an overall wonderful person. Big up Brooksy, Diolch.

Davinder Sanghera for looking out for me like a big sister, supporting me and giving me blunt advice that always makes me a better property investor.

Rubi for the endless energy that she radiates, **James** for being the best uncle ji ever, **Dee** for advising me on correcting my mistakes, **Adam** for the laughter, **Gurpreet** for the spirituality, **Ope** for the good vibes

Tej Talks

& Zanku, **Ade** for the consistent positive support and **Amanda** for the Skincare chats.

To all my Investors, for believing in me and supporting me to achieve my ambitions and sticking with me when things were delayed.

To all the great tradespeople who have helped me so much.

Thanks to those event hosts/organisers who invite me to speak at their events.

To the following people in no particular order for reading various sections of my book and providing invaluable feedback and critiques:

Paul Million (& Kids), Josh Asquith, Rubi Takhar, James Sahota, Gurpreet Kaur, Ayaz Saboor, Adebayo Adebisi, Anika Vaghela, Terry Tumba, Suresh Nath, Rob Hodge, Mohit Mehta, Sandi Aulakh, Rhys Morgan, Jay Howard, Ope Adeoshun, Daniel Baines, Jasmine Dosanjh, Priya Kripalani, Harley and Guy, Viraj and Priyanka Patel, Adam Rana, Amanda Clarke, Davinder Sanghera, Andrew Elite, David Morgan-Kane, Dan Hulbert, Martin Rapley, Sam Spencer, George Dugard, Cate Brooks, and Richard Liddle.

Tej Talks

Thank you, for purchasing and reading this book, oh and for the Amazon review you're obviously about to leave me! *hint, hint*

One more case study? Go on!
[CASE STUDY 6] – 55CRD

Purchase Price: £28,000 (No SDLT)
Conveyancing Fee: £600
Auction Fee: £375
Refurbishment: £15,200
Freehold Purchase: £12,000
Interest on Finance: £2,970

Total money in: £59,840

RICS Valuation: £70,000

Remortgage Amount (75% LTV): £52,500

Money left in: £7,340

Monthly
Rent: £500
Mortgage Cost: £153
Insurance Cost: £15
Cash flow/Profit: £332

Annual Cashflow/Profit: £3,984
ROCLI: 50%

Purchased at auction, vendor had it empty for 7 years. Had wild dreams for it. I purchased the freehold, made it into a sexy 2 bed with a feature window and got a lower value than expected, but it still fits my ROCLI.